D1994816

STARK

TRAINING ENGLISCH

Ariane Last

Englisch 6. Klasse

Aufgaben mit Lösungen

Hauptschule

STARK

ISBN 978-3-86668-658-8

Inhalt

Fortsetzung siehe nächste Seite

Autorin: Ariane Last
Illustratorin: Rebecca Meyer

Vorwort an die Schüler

Liebe Schülerin, lieber Schüler,

Englisch ist eine Sprache, mit der man sich in vielen Teilen der Welt verständigen kann, nicht nur in England oder den USA. Du willst nach dem Weg fragen, Essen im Restaurant bestellen oder einfach nur ein nettes Gespräch führen – sowohl im Urlaub als auch später im Berufsleben wird dir Englisch oft nützlich sein. Doch auch im Deutschen gebrauchst du viele englische Wörter, z. B. „Laptop“ oder „Skateboard“. Darüber hinaus ist das Internet voller englischer Begriffe wie „Download“ oder „Homepage“. Du siehst, wie wichtig es ist, Englisch zu verstehen und zu sprechen.

Die **Texte**, **Erklärungen**, **Beispiele und Übungen** in diesem Buch helfen dir dabei, dein **Grundwissen** im Fach Englisch zu trainieren. Wichtige Themen und Regeln, die du im Unterricht kennenlernst, werden hier behandelt.

- Jedes Kapitel beginnt mit einem **Text** und Aufgaben zum **Leseverstehen**. Es erwarten dich viele Geschichten und Informationen zum Alltagsleben englischer Kinder aus Greenwich, einem Stadtteil Londons.
- Es folgt jeweils eine kurze Erklärung zu einer **Grammatikregel** mit passenden Beispielsätzen. Anhand einfacher und etwas schwierigerer Aufgaben kannst du die Grammatikregeln dann anwenden.
- In jedem Kapitel findest du außerdem eine oder mehrere Übungen zu den Bereichen **Wortschatz** und **Schreiben**.
- Die **Lösungen** zu den Übungen findest du im **„Key“** am Ende des Buches.
- Du findest außerdem ein **Vokabelverzeichnis**, das dir diejenigen Wörter aus dem Buch erklärt, die du vielleicht noch nicht kennst oder die du vergessen hast. Du kannst damit aber auch deinen Wortschatz erweitern.

Dieses Übungsbuch musst du nicht gleich ganz durcharbeiten. Du kannst auch immer nur das Kapitel bearbeiten, das den Stoff beinhaltet, der gerade im Unterricht behandelt wird. Auch vor Proben bzw. Klassenarbeiten kannst du einzelne Kapitel wiederholen. Eine weitere Möglichkeit wäre, das Buch zur Wiederholung von bestimmten Themen (z. B. „School“) zu nutzen. Wiederhole die Aufgaben auch immer nach einer Weile, um deine Kenntnisse zu festigen.

Ich wünsche dir viel Spaß und Erfolg bei der Arbeit mit diesem Buch!

Ariane Last

Vorwort an die Eltern

Liebe Eltern,

die Grundlagen der englischen Sprache hat Ihr Kind bereits im vergangenen Schuljahr gelegt. Dieses Buch greift einige Themen aus Klasse 5 wieder auf und vertieft sie mit neuem Wortschatz. Des Weiteren werden neue grammatikalische Strukturen der 6. Jahrgangsstufe kleinschrittig eingeführt und mit vertiefenden Übungen gefestigt.

- Der **gesamte Stoff der 6. Klasse** wird verständlich erklärt und mithilfe von Beispielen veranschaulicht. Anhand von abwechslungsreichen **Aufgaben** können die jeweiligen Inhalte dann systematisch trainiert werden. Der Stoff richtet sich nach den aktuellen Lehrplänen der verschiedenen Bundesländer und ist damit breit gefächert.
- Zu Beginn jedes Kapitels steht immer ein kurzer **Text**, der meist vom Alltag mehrerer fiktiver Schülerinnen und Schüler aus dem Londoner Stadtteil Greenwich handelt. Danach folgen Übungen zu den Kompetenzbereichen **Leseverstehen**, **Grammatik**, **Wortschatz** und **Schreiben**.
- Die Übungen umfassen verschiedene Schwierigkeitsgrade, von einfach bis anspruchsvoll. Zahlreiche **Bilder und Illustrationen** fördern den Lernprozess und bringen Freude beim Lernen.
- Erst nach der Bearbeitung einer Aufgabe sollte Ihr Kind die **Lösungen** im Lösungsteil („Key“) ansehen. Kennzeichnen Sie die Bereiche, die Ihrem Kind noch schwerfallen, damit Sie wissen, was es noch besonders üben müsste.
- Nicht nur das Erlernen der Sprachstruktur ist für Ihr Kind wichtig, sondern auch die Erweiterung seines englischen **Wortschatzes**. In diesem Buch kommen auch einige Wörter vor, die Ihr Kind noch nicht kennt. Damit wird trainiert, wie man die Bedeutung unbekannter Wörter mithilfe von Bildern oder aus dem Zusammenhang erschließt – eine Fähigkeit, die für den Gebrauch einer Fremdsprache unerlässlich ist. Außerdem findet sich am Schluss des Buches ein umfassendes **Vokabelverzeichnis** zum Nachschlagen und Wiederholen. So wird Ihr Kind auch an den Umgang mit einem Wörterbuch herangeführt.

Ich wünsche Ihnen und Ihrem Kind viel Erfolg!

Ariane Last

Topics and worksheets

In den folgenden Kapiteln findest du Texte mit Aufgaben zu unterschiedlichen Themen. Jedes Kapitel enthält Aufgaben aus den Bereichen **Leseverstehen**, **Grammatik**, **Wortschatz** und **Schreiben**. Du musst aber nicht alle Kapitel und alle Bereiche der Reihe nach durcharbeiten. Sieh einfach im Inhaltsverzeichnis nach, was du besonders üben möchtest.

Topic 1: My dream life

On the first day after the summer holidays the boys and girls in Year 8 talk about their dream lives. Here is what some pupils say.

Simon

In my dream life I wake up late every day. I eat a lot of sweets and I don't tidy up my room. I stay there all day and watch DVDs, play video games and listen to loud music. My best friends often visit me and we stay up all night.

Carl

I live in California and I do lots of extreme sports every day. In the mornings I dive with sharks or swim with dolphins in the ocean. In the afternoons I meet my best friends and we go windsurfing. And in the evenings there is still enough time for indoor climbing.

Lila

My dream is to have a big family with at least four children. We live in a nice house at the sea where we often swim and sail. At the weekends we meet our friends and have a barbecue and play games.

Sarah

There's no school in my dream life. So I travel around the world. I start in Europe and then fly to Asia. I don't know its culture but I think it's interesting. I also want to spend some time in South America. I'd like to camp in the rainforest.

Fragen zum Text

1 Wie sieht das Wunschleben der Schülerinnen und Schüler aus? Lies die Texte und verbinde die Namen mit dem jeweils passenden Bild.

Lila

Carl

Simon

Sarah

2 Als Hausaufgabe soll die Klasse einen Tagebucheintrag über einen Tag in ihrem Wunschleben schreiben. Welchen Text könnten die vier Schüler jeweils geschrieben haben? Schreibe ihren Namen auf das richtige Blatt Papier.

Name:

... A safari trip is great! You see lions, giraffes or hippos. Next week I will be in Canada to ski or in New York to go shopping ...

Name:

... Dancing is so much fun. My teacher is fantastic. He knows all the new moves by Usher ...

Name:

... What a lazy day. It's evening now and I don't know what to do. I know all my films and I am bored of my PC games ... I think I'll ask my friends to come over ...

Name:

... I like to help sick people. Being a doctor is my dream job. The hospital where I work is new and very close to my home ...

Name:

... It is a lot of fun to swim with dolphins. They are such beautiful and intelligent animals! ...

Name:

... It's my daughter's fifth birthday today. We're having a surprise party for her in the garden. In the afternoon the children will go swimming ...

Grammatik

Wann verwendest du das *simple present*?

Du verwendest das *simple present* (Gegenwart) vor allem,

- wenn du ausdrücken willst, dass jemand etwas mag oder nicht mag.
  Beispiel: Mary likes her new dress. *Mary gefällt ihr neues Kleid.*
- wenn Ereignisse regelmäßig stattfinden.
  Beispiel: I go swimming every Friday. *Ich gehe jeden Freitag schwimmen.*

Zusammen mit dem *simple present* stehen oft Wörter und Ausdrücke, die dir sagen, **wie oft etwas geschieht**, zum Beispiel: *every day, sometimes, always, never, often*

Beispiel: She gets up at 6 o'clock every day.
Sie steht jeden Tag um 6 Uhr auf.

Wie bildest du das *simple present*?

- Nach ***I / you / we / they*** behält das Verb (Tunwort) seine Grundform.
  Nach ***he / she / it*** wird an die Grundform die **Endung -s** angehängt.

1. Person Singular	I like swimming.	*Ich schwimme gerne.*
2. Person Singular	You like swimming.	*Du schwimmst gerne./ Sie schwimmen gerne.* (Höflichkeitsform)
3. Person Singular	He likes swimming.	*Er schwimmt gerne.*
	She likes swimming.	*Sie schwimmt gerne.*
	It likes swimming.	*Es schwimmt gerne.*

Merke: *He, she, it* – **s** muss mit!

1. Person Plural	We like swimming.	*Wir schwimmen gerne.*
2. Person Plural	You like swimming.	*Ihr schwimmt gerne./ Sie schwimmen gerne.* (Höflichkeitsform)
3. Person Plural	They like swimming.	*Sie schwimmen gerne.*

Bei manchen Wörtern wird jedoch die Endung **-es** oder **-ies** angehängt:
Beispiele: do → does watch → watches go → goes carry → carries

3 Was machen die Schüler in ihrem Wunschleben? Verwende das *simple present.*

a Simon: "I eat chocolate and crisps for lunch."
Simon eats chocolate and crisps for lunch.

b Tom: "I play football for Manchester United."

____

c Carl: “In the evenings I go climbing.”

____

d Lila: “I swim with my children in the sea.”

____

e Sarah: “In the cities I see many famous sights.”

____

f Jenny: “I am a doctor and help people.”

____

g Arthur: “To keep fit I do some sport before breakfast.”

____

4 Was machen die Schüler in ihrem echten Leben? Bilde mit den vorgegebenen Satzteilen für jeden Tag der Woche einen Satz in der *simple-present*-Form. Verbinde die Satzteile zuerst und schreibe die Sätze dann auf.

Monday	Simon and Lisa	take the dog for a walk
Tuesday	Carl	go to the cinema
Wednesday	Lila and Lucy	surf the Internet
Thursday	Sarah	hang out with friends
Friday	Tom and Jerry	listen to music
Saturday	Jenny	read magazines
Sunday	Arthur and Barry	draw pictures

On Monday Sarah listens to music.

On Tuesday ______________________________

On ______________________________

____

____

____

____

Wie bildest du verneinte Sätze im *simple present*?

Nach ***I / you / we / they*** stellst du ***don't (do not)*** vor die Grundform des Verbs.
Nach ***he / she / it*** stellst du ***doesn't (does not)*** vor die Grundform des Verbs.

	Langform	Kurzform
1. Person Singular	I do not swim.	I don't swim.
2. Person Singular	You do not swim.	You don't swim.
3. Person Singular	He does not swim.	He doesn't swim.
	She does not swim.	She doesn't swim.
	It does not swim.	It doesn't swim.
1. Person Plural	We do not swim.	We don't swim.
2. Person Plural	You do not swim.	You don't swim.
3. Person Plural	They do not swim.	They don't swim.

5 Vervollständige die folgenden Sätze mit den richtigen Wörtern aus dem Kasten. Der erste Satz ist immer verneint.

live	smell	~~watch~~	tidy up	meet	eat	go

a Dominic _doesn't watch_ sad movies. He _watches_ funny movies. *(ansehen)*

b Livia ______________ in Berlin. She ______________ in Cologne. *(wohnen)*

c We ______________ meat. We only ______________ vegetables. *(essen)*

d Your clothes ______________ nice. They ______________ bad. *(riechen)*

e John ______________ to school by train. He and a friend ______________ by bus. *(fahren)*

f I ______________________ my girlfriend in the city. I ______________ her at home. *(treffen)*

g Anthony's mum ____________________________ his room. Anthony _________________ his room himself. *(aufräumen)*

Wie bildest du Fragen im *simple present*?

- Bei Fragen mit ***I / you / we / they*** wird **Do** an den Anfang des Satzes gestellt:
  Beispiele: You go swimming. — Do you go swimming?
  They like football. — Do they like football?
- Bei Fragen mit ***he / she / it*** wird **Does** an den Anfang des Satzes gestellt:
  Beispiele: He goes swimming. — Does he go swimming?
  She likes football. — Does she like football?
- **Kurzantworten** bildest du folgendermaßen:
  Do you like London? — Yes, I do. / No, I don't.
  Does she like London? — Yes, she does. / No, she doesn't.

6 Sieh dir die Wochenübersicht der Schüler genau an. Vervollständige die Fragen und gib passende Kurzantworten.

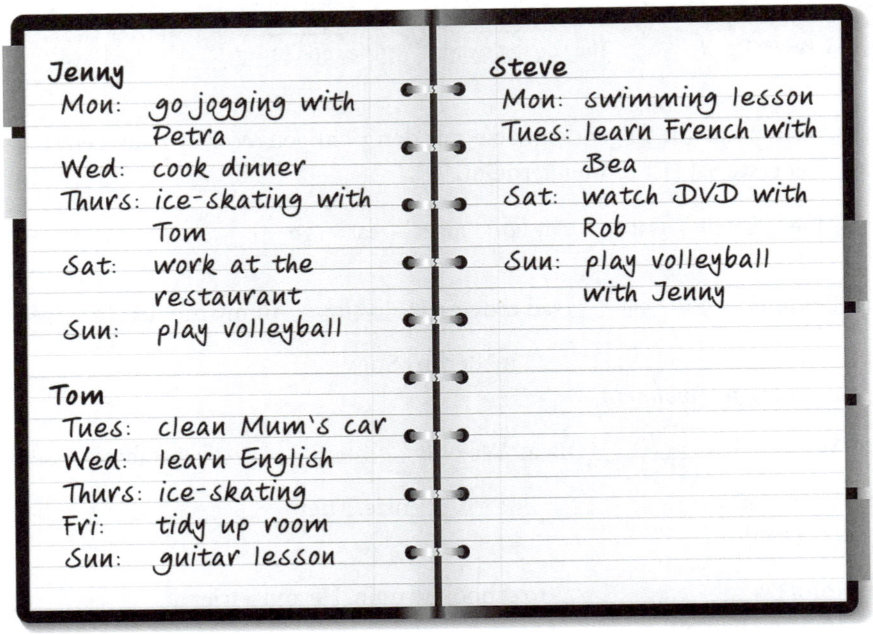

a Does Jenny cook dinner on Wednesday? – Yes, she does.

b ________ Tom play the guitar? – ______, he ____________.

c ________ Jenny go ice-skating on Monday? – ______, she ____________.

d ________ Steve and Rob watch DVDs? – ______, they ____________.

e ________ Jenny play hockey? – ________, ______________.

f ________ Bea and Steve learn French? – ________, ______________.

g ________ Tom and Jenny play volleyball together?

– ______, ______________________________.

h ________ Tom clean his mum's car on Thursday?

– ______, ______________________________.

7 Das ist Mika vom Planeten Meratan. Bei einer Reise zur Erde fiel ihm auf, dass die Menschen seltsamen Freizeitaktivitäten nachgehen. Seinen Freunden zeigt er Fotos, die die Erdlinge bei ihren Lieblingsbeschäftigungen zeigen. Setze die richtigen Formen des *simple present* in die Lücken ein.

a FRIENDS: ______ the earthlings also ____________ spaceball?

MIKA: No, ______________. They ____________ ______________.

b FRIENDS: ______ the earthlings also ____________ in slime?

MIKA: No, __________. ______________ in water.

c FRIENDS: __________ a child from planet Earth also like to __________ worms?

MIKA: A child from planet Earth ______________ worms! The children like to ______________ ______________, for example.

d MIKA: The earthlings ______________ space ships. They ______________.

e MIKA: The earthlings like to ______________ music.
FRIENDS: What is music? We ______________ know what that is.

Wortschatz

8 Mika möchte wissen, welche seltsamen Hobbys die Menschen noch ausüben. Schreibe ein paar für ihn auf. Unten findest du einige Beispiele. Du kannst aber auch noch andere Hobbys auflisten.

Many people on earth like to …

– *play chess (Schach)*

– *collect …*

____

____

____

Schreiben

9 Vervollständige das folgende Gedicht. Sieh dir aber zuerst das Bild an: wie könnte der Titel des Gedichts lauten?

My __________ does my ____________________

Fülle nun die Lücken im Gedicht mit den Wörtern aus dem Kasten.

question night dog and homework (2 x) work one right

My __________ does my ____________________ at home
every __________.
He answers each ____________________
__________ gets them all __________.
There's only __________ problem with ____________________ by Rover.
I can't turn in __________ that's been slobbered all over.

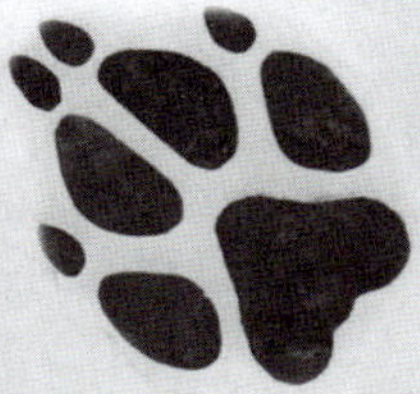

Topic 2: Back to school

Today is the first day of school after the summer holidays. Tessa is a new girl in Year 8. It is lunch break now and Sue from her class is showing her around:

SUE: This is our cafeteria. You can have a snack here every lunch break. Today most pupils are eating pizza. You can get drinks over there if you like. Look, they are also selling ice-cream this afternoon.

TESSA: I love ice-cream!

SUE: And after lunch some pupils go outside. Look, Peter and Sam are playing basketball now. They often do that.

TESSA: I'm in a basketball club. I usually go there on Mondays and Fridays.

SUE: Why don't you go to the school club? They always meet on Wednesday evening. This is the coach, Mr Miller. He's in the gym most of the time.

TESSA: Good idea. I can ask him later.

SUE: And this is our new library. At the moment Kim is reading a book. She's in our class, too. Kim, do you know where Paula and Fred are?

KIM: Hi, Sue. Paula is singing karaoke in the music room. And Fred is helping Mrs Dough in the school kiosk right now.

SUE: Thanks. The kiosk always opens at 8.30 a.m. and closes at 3 p.m. from Monday to Friday. Come on, Tessa. Let's buy something!

Fragen zum Text

10 Lies dir den Text genau durch und kreuze dann das richtige Bild zur jeweiligen Frage an.

a Where do the pupils eat their lunch?

b What is Tessa's favourite dessert?

c Mr Miller is the coach of which team?

d What is Paula doing?

11 Lies dir den Text noch einmal durch und vervollständige die Sätze.

a Pupils can have a snack every ______________________.

b Peter and Sam often ______________________.

c Tessa usually does sports on ______________ and ______________.

d The school club doesn't meet in the afternoon.
They meet ______________________.

e Kim ______________________ a book in the library.

f In the ______________________ you can sing karaoke.

g Mrs Dough works ______________________.

h The kiosk isn't ______________________ at the weekend.

Grammatik

Wann verwendest du das *present progressive?*

Du benutzt das ***present progressive*** (Verlaufsform der Gegenwart), um auszudrücken, was zum Zeitpunkt des Sprechens **gerade geschieht**. Im Deutschen drückst du dies mit Adverbien wie „gerade" aus.

Beispiele: He is cooking. — *Er kocht gerade.*
They are cooking. — *Sie kochen gerade.*

Signalwörter für das *present progressive* sind z. B. *at the moment, (right) now*

12 Schreibe fünf *present-progressive*-Formen aus dem Text auf.

present progressive

Wie bildest du die *progressive*-Form (*-ing*-Form)?

sing	–	singing	Im Normalfall: Verb + *-ing*
sit	–	sitting	Wenn der vorausgehende Vokal kurz ist und die letzte Silbe betont wird: Verdoppelung des Konsonanten
write	–	writing	Wenn das Verb mit einem *-e* endet, so fällt dieses weg.
lie	–	lying	Aus *-ie* am Ende des Verbs wird *-y*.

Wie bildest du das *present progressive*?

- Du bildest das *present progressive*, indem du nach das Subjekt (Satzgegenstand) die folgenden Formen stellst: **Form von *be* + Verb in der *-ing*-Form**.

I am watching TV.	*Ich sehe fern.*
You are watching TV.	*Du siehst fern. / Sie sehen fern.* (Höflichkeitsform)
He/She/It is watching TV.	*Er/Sie/Es sieht fern.*
We are watching TV.	*Wir sehen fern.*
You are watching TV.	*Ihr seht fern. / Sie sehen fern.* (Höflichkeitsform)
They are watching TV.	*Sie sehen fern.*

- In der Umgangssprache werden auch die **Kurzformen** verwendet:
  Beispiele: I'm watching TV.
  He's watching TV.
  You're watching TV.

13 Was geschieht auf den Bildern gerade? Vervollständige die Sätze im *present progressive*.

a A pupil ________ reading a book.

b The pupils ________ listening to the teacher.

c John is ______________________________ a text message on his mobile phone.

d A man and a woman ______ __________ out of the train window.

e The boy ______ _______________ during the lesson.

f Zoe and Steve ______ __________ __________________.

Wie bildest du die Verneinung im *present progressive*?

Verneinte Sätze, in denen das ***present progressive*** verwendet wird, bildest du folgendermaßen: **Form von *to be* + *not* + Verb in der *ing*-Form**

I am not watching TV.	(I'm not watching TV.)	*Ich sehe nicht fern.*
You are not watching TV.	(You're not watching TV.)	*Du siehst nicht fern. / Sie sehen nicht fern.*
He/She/It is not watching TV.	(He/She/It isn't watching TV.)	*Er/Sie/Es sieht nicht fern.*
We are not watching TV.	(We aren't watching TV.)	*Wir sehen nicht fern.*
You are not watching TV.	(You aren't watching TV.)	*Ihr seht nicht fern. / Sie sehen nicht fern.*
They are not watching TV.	(They aren't watching TV.)	*Sie sehen nicht fern.*

Wenn du diese Form benutzt, kannst du sagen, was gerade **nicht** passiert.

14 Was machen die Schüler nicht? Schreibe einen negativen Satz im *present progressive*.

a Tim is writing a story. He _is not / isn't writing_ an e-mail.

b Vera and Meg are cleaning their bikes.

They ______________________________ their mopeds.

c Kim is opening the door. She ______________________ the window.

d Dad and I ______________________ in the garden.
We are working in the garage.

e I ______________________ Spanish.
I am learning French and English.

f You are drawing a farm.
You ______________________ a city.

g Tina is arriving home at 7 pm.
She ______________________ home at 7 am.

Wie bildest du Fragen im *present progressive?*

Fragesätze, in denen das ***present progressive*** verwendet wird, bildest du, indem du die **Form von *to be* an den Satzanfang** stellst:

Beispiele:	You are reading.	Are you reading?	*Liest du gerade?*
	He is reading.	Is he reading?	*Liest er gerade?*

Kurzantworten bildest du folgendermaßen:

Beispiele:	Are you reading?	Yes, I am. / No, I am not. / I'm not.
	Is he reading?	Yes, he is. / No, he is not. / he isn't.

Beachte: Nur in der verneinten Antwort kannst du die Kurzformen des *present progressive* verwenden.

15 Es ist Wochenende. Was machen die Schüler gerade? Bilde Fragen im *present progressive* und beantworte sie in Form von Kurzantworten.

a Are you riding a horse? (ride a horse) – ☺ Yes, I am.

b ________ we ______________________ now? (go to the cinema)
☺ Yes, ______________.

c ________ you ______________________? (buy a skirt)
☹ No, ______________.

d ________ Felix ______________________? (play with a friend)
☺ Yes, ______________.

e ________ Emma and Terry ______________________? (enjoy the trip)
☹ No, ______________.

16 Die erste Schulwoche ist vorbei und Sue ruft ihre Tante an, um ihr von der Schule zu berichten. Schreibe die jeweils richtige *present-progressive*-Form in die Lücken. Verwende so oft wie möglich die Kurzformen.

SUE: Hi Aunt Sally. How are you? I ______________ (call) to tell you about my first day back at school.

AUNT: Hello, my dear. Thanks for calling. Any news?

SUE: There's a new girl called Tessa in my class. She's very nice and plays basketball. Our school team ______________________ (look) for new players. Maybe she can join the club. Anyway, what are ______________ ______________ (do) right now?

AUNT: I ______________________ (clean) the bathroom and your uncle ______________________ (work) outside. There is always something to do in the garden.

SUE: I know. Dad ______________________ (cut) the bushes at the moment. And Mum ______________________ (go) to town now.

AUNT: Why ______ she ______________ (go) to town?

SUE: She needs a nice dress for tomorrow night. There's a festival.

AUNT: Oh, nice. And you ______________________ (not help) your dad?

SUE: No, I __________, I don't have time. Chloe, a friend from school, ______________________ (wait) for me. We ______________________ (write) a report about a new computer game.

AUNT: OK, my love. Thanks for your call.

SUE: You're welcome. Bye bye.

Wortschatz

17 Tessa überträgt ihren neuen Stundenplan für ihre Mutter. Bisher hat sie nur kleine Bilder in die einzelnen Felder gemalt. Die Fächer stehen auf ihrem Notizzettel. Hilf ihr, die Felder zu beschriften.

German Geography History Art Science English
Physical Education (P.E.) Maths Music Information Technology (IT)

TIMETABLE

NAME: *Tessa Owen* YEAR: *8*

Monday	Tuesday	Wednesday	Thursday	Friday

				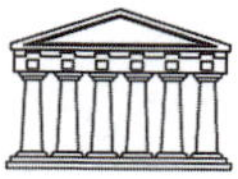
LUNCH BREAK				

18 Tessa hat einige Räume ihrer neuen Schule fotografiert, um sie ihrer Familie zu zeigen. Kannst du sie benennen? Wenn du die Buchstaben in die richtige Reihenfolge bringst, verraten sie dir die Lösung.

alcrmooss

mgy

titleos

rmoocmopetur

icftearea

cmiusomor

yblirar

iktnehc

dnegar

Schreiben

19 Tessa schreibt ihrer besten Freundin eine E-Mail über ihren ersten Tag an der neuen Schule. Fülle die Lücken mit den passenden Wörtern aus.

Untitled - Message (Plain Text)

File Edit View Insert Format Tools Actions Help

Send | Accounts | Options...

To...

Cc...

Bcc...

Subject:

Hi Linda,

I want to tell you about my first ____________ at my new school. Mrs Glinn is my favourite ________________. She teaches ____________ in our class one day a week. You know it's my favourite ____________________. I love painting and drawing pictures!

The school is really good. There's a big _________________ where you can sit and read books. Right now I _______________________________ this mail to you in the ________________________. It is very modern and you can surf the Internet whenever you like. During break you can ____________ football or other games outside. Next week I'm going to the _________________________ club. I'm so excited! And I've got a new friend. Her ________________ is Sue. She is really nice.

Take care!

Love, Tessa

Topic 3: Who was it?

It's Saturday afternoon. Simon and two other boys from Year 8 are doing an interview on Greenwich High Street for a school project. Suddenly two police cars stop in front of the shopping centre: A woman has stolen a diamond ring from the jeweller's shop and has run away. Here is what some people told the police:

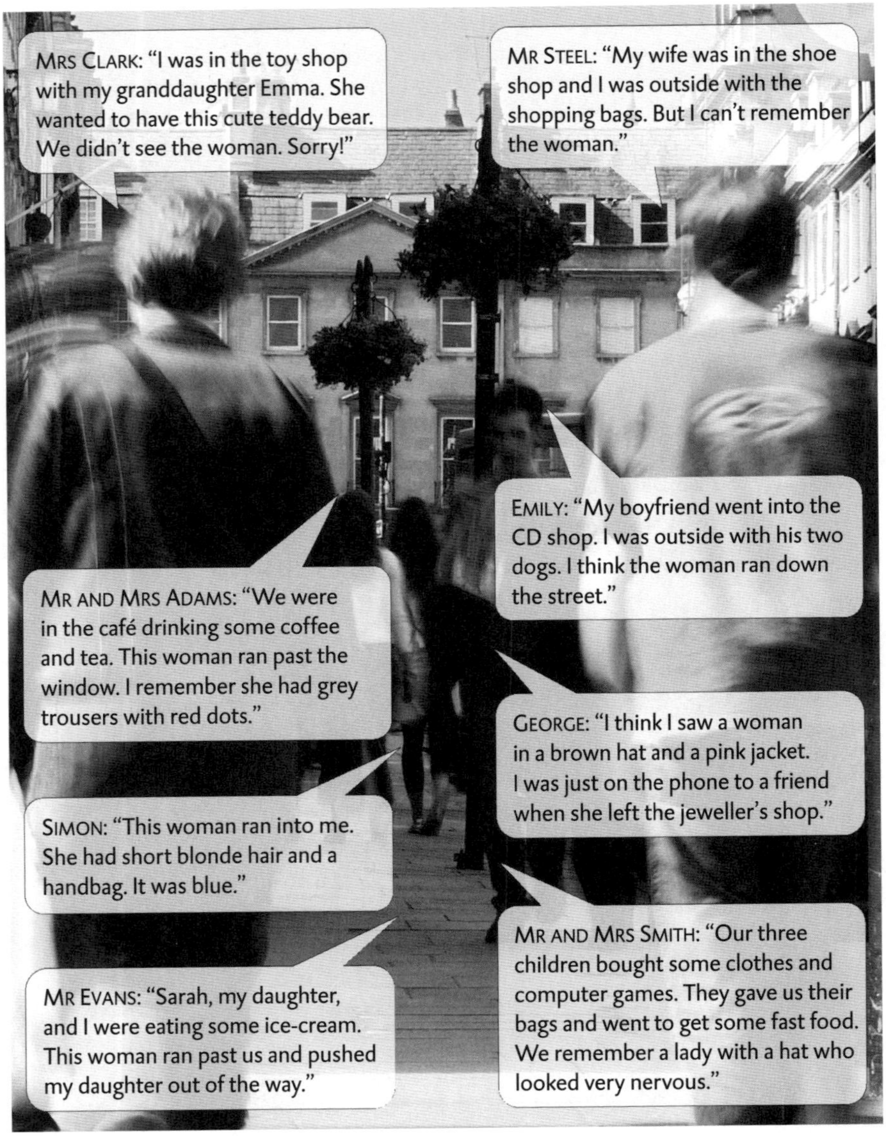

Fragen zum Text

20 Hier siehst du einige Leute, die vor dem Einkaufszentrum von der Polizei befragt wurden. Wie heißen die abgebildeten Personen? Schreibe ihre Namen in die Kästchen.

21 Hier ist ein Phantombild der Diebin. Vervollständige es mithilfe der Zeugenaussagen und male es auch in den richtigen Farben aus.

22 Lies die Texte noch einmal durch. Welche Aussagen sind richtig? Hake sie ab.

- [ ] Sarah bought a teddy bear.
- [ ] Mrs Smith has got three children.
- [ ] Mrs Clark is Emma's grandma.
- [ ] Emily's boyfriend has got three dogs.
- [ ] Mrs Steel was in the shoe shop.
- [ ] Mr Evans ate fast food in the shopping centre.
- [ ] The woman ran into Simon.
- [ ] Mr Steel drank tea in a café.

Grammatik

Welche Personalpronomen (Persönliche Fürwörter) in der Subjektform gibt es?

Du kennst bereits die Subjektformen der englischen Personalpronomen:

1. Person Singular	I *(ich)*	*1. Person Plural*	we *(wir)*
2. Person Singular	you *(du/Sie)*	*2. Person Plural*	you *(ihr/Sie)*
3. Person Singular	he, she, it *(er, sie, es)*	*3. Person Plural*	they *(sie)*

Die Subjektform der Personalpronomen kann ein Nomen (Namenwort) ersetzen, das Subjekt (Satzgegenstand) eines Satzes ist.

Beispiel: Susan is at home. She is listening to music.

23 Setze das jeweils richtige Personalpronomen für die unterstrichenen Satzteile ein.

a Tom's favourite music is hip hop. *He* listens to music all day.

b Greg and Joshua play the guitar. ________ meet three times a week.

c Evie is a music fan, but ________ can't play an instrument.

d Everyone listens to Radio FM 105. ________ plays a lot of popular songs.

e A friend and I are going to a concert. ________ got the tickets for Christmas.

f The two girls are good at playing the piano. ________ practise a lot.

g Hannah asks Tom: "Do ________ want to dance?"

h Lisa's friend Simon likes sports. ________ always watches football on TV.

24 Schreibe zu jeder Frage die passende Antwort. Es gibt mehr Antworten zur Auswahl als Fragen.

a How old are Ethan and Evie?

____

b Is blue your favourite colour?

____

c Where is Millie today?

____

d Ben and Jerry, are you ready for dinner?

____

e Would you like to visit me?

____

No, it's not true.

I would love to.

He's older.

She is at her aunt's house.

I'm at home.

They're bigger.

Yes, we're so hungry!

Yes, we do.

Yes, it is.

They're twelve years old.

Welche Personalpronomen (Persönliche Fürwörter) in der Objektform gibt es?

Die Objektformen der englischen Personalpronomen lauten:

1. Person Singular	me	*(mir, mich)*	*1. Person Plural*	us	*(uns)*
2. Person Singular	you	*(dir/Ihnen, dich/Sie)*	*2. Person Plural*	you	*(euch/Ihnen, sie/Sie)*
3. Person Singular	him	*(ihm, ihn)*	*3. Person Plural*	them	*(ihnen, sie)*
	her	*(ihr, sie)*			
	it	*(ihm, es)*			

Wann verwendest du die Objektformen der Personalpronomen?

Die Objektform der Personalpronomen kann ein Nomen (Namenwort) ersetzen, das Objekt (Satzergänzung) eines Satzes ist.

Beispiele: Susan likes Tom. Mary likes him, too.
Susan mag Tom. Mary mag ihn auch.

Can you help mum? Yes, I can help her.
Kannst du Mama helfen? Ja, ich kann ihr helfen.

Beachte: Im Englischen sind die Formen für den Dativ (wem?) und den Akkusativ (wen?) gleich:

Beispiele: I can help her. *Ich kann ihr helfen.* *(Wem kann ich helfen?)*
I can see her. *Ich kann sie sehen.* *(Wen kann ich sehen?)*

25 Welches Objektpronomen kann man für den unterstrichenen Satzteil einsetzen? Kreuze das richtige Wort an.

a Clara explains the exercise to <u>her friend Louise</u>.

☐ us ☐ me ☑ her

b They don't know <u>the film</u>.

☐ it ☐ you ☐ them

c Ann is writing an e-mail to <u>Fred</u>.

☐ her ☐ me ☐ him

d Yesterday Theo called <u>Jane</u>.

☐ him ☐ it ☐ her

e Grandma bought some sweets for <u>her grandchildren</u>.

☐ us ☐ you ☐ them

f Close <u>the door</u>, please.

☐ her ☐ it ☐ them

g Can you show <u>my brother and me</u> how it works?

☐ you ☐ us ☐ them

26 Setze jeweils das richtige Objektpronomen ein.

a Where is Liam? Have you seen _him_?

b Phoebe and Oscar have got some new games. They often play ________.

c "Daisy, can I come with ________. I've missed the bus."

d We're at home tonight. Sue can call ________.

e Megan is a good friend of mine. I like ________ a lot.

f I'm going to town. Do you want to come with ________?

g Teacher: "Max and Jake, I can hear ________ talking!"

h "Believe ________, I know where to go."

Wortschatz

27 In der Stadt gibt es viele Geschäfte. Um welche Geschäfte und Orte handelt es sich auf den Schildern? Schreibe den jeweils richtigen Begriff aus dem Kasten neben die Bilder. Es gibt mehr Begriffe, als du brauchst.

market post office restaurant café car park shoe shop bookshop butcher bakery pet shop

Schreiben

28 Eine ältere Dame ist gerade am Bahnhof in Greenwich angekommen. Sie kennt sich in der Stadt nicht aus und fragt dich nach dem Weg. Sieh dir den Stadtplan an und beschreibe ihr den Weg. Die folgenden Wörter helfen dir dabei:

turn left/right	go straight on	go along	cross
next to	opposite	on the left/right	

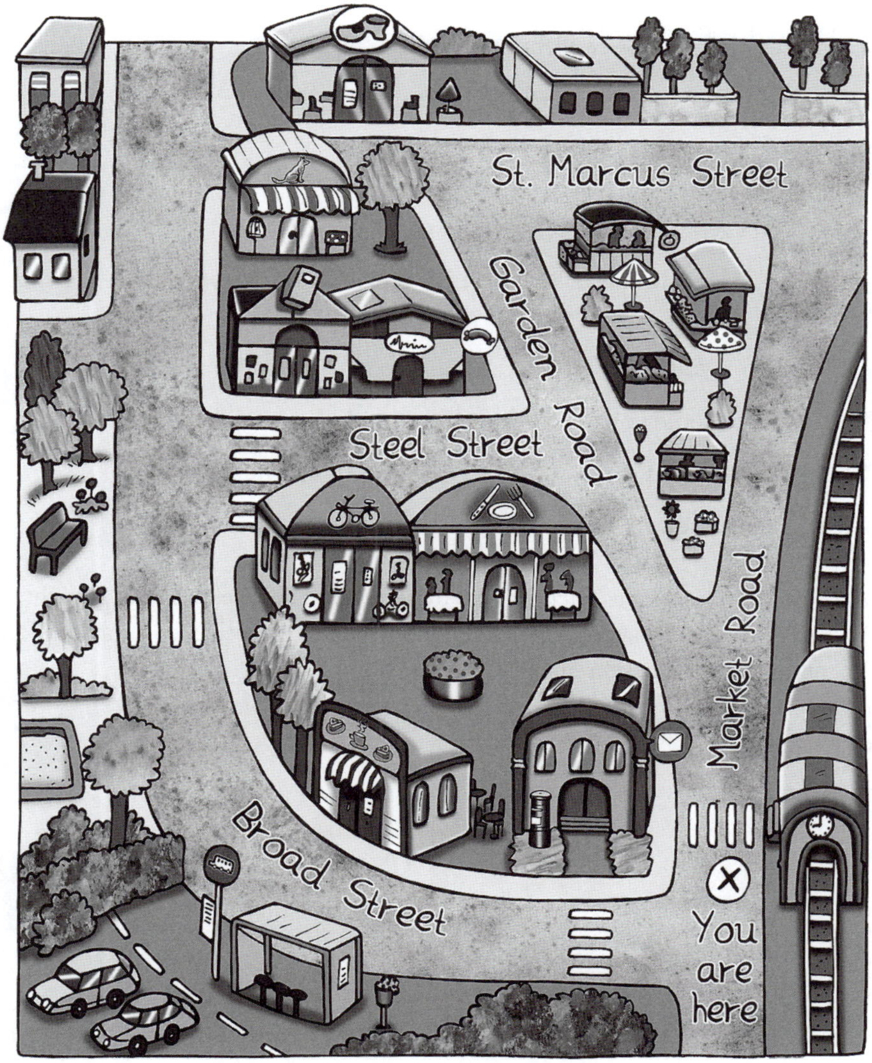

LADY: Excuse me, maybe you can help me. How do I get to the bus stop where the buses to the city centre stop?

YOU: Well, you ____

____

____

____.

LADY: Oh, thank you. I'm going to see my granddaughter and I would like to bring her a book. Is there also a book shop nearby?

YOU: Yes, there is. We're at the station now, and you ____________________

____

____

____.

LADY: Can I get a coffee there?

YOU: No, I don't think so. But there is a café in Broad Street. ______________

______________________________________ until you see the café on your left.

LADY: Great! Could you tell me how to get to the bus stop from the café?

YOU: That's easy. It's just ____________________ the café.

LADY: Thank you very much.

29 Für eine Fahndung ist es wichtig, das Aussehen und die Kleidung der gesuchten Person möglichst genau darzustellen. Mit welchen Eigenschaften kannst du die folgenden Begriffe beschreiben?

hair	body	clothes	face
•	• athletic	•	• small nose
•	•	•	•
•	•	•	•
•	•	•	•
•	•	•	•

30 Die Polizei hat zwei Fahndungsbilder von Dieben veröffentlicht. Nutze die Wörter aus Aufgabe 29 und schreibe zu einem Bild einen passenden Fahndungstext.

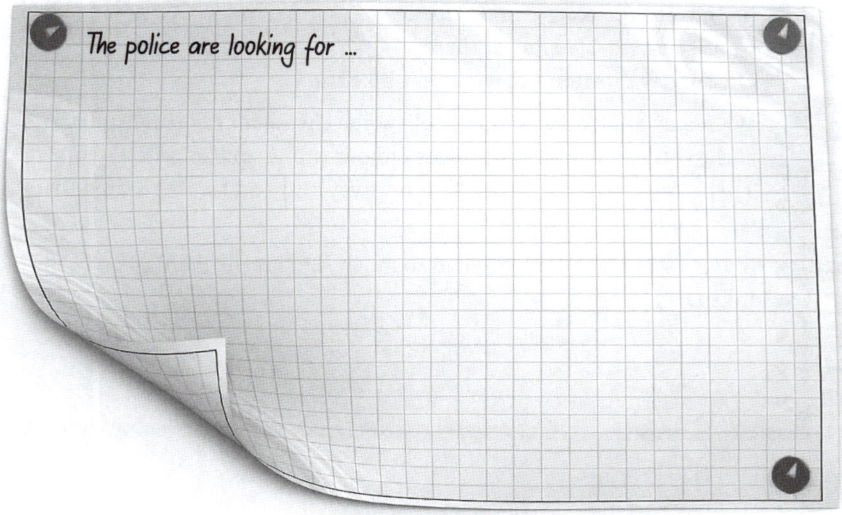

Topic 4: A trip to the Lake District

Sue and her parents invited Tessa on a weekend trip to the Lake District – a national park in the north of England. On Sunday evening Tessa wrote in her diary:

Dear Diary,

We started our tour on Friday afternoon. In the evening we arrived at the cottage. After dinner we played some board games and talked for a long time.

On Saturday morning we hiked to the top of the highest mountain in the Lake District. It was sunny and we had a great view. It was fantastic! We took some pictures and walked down again. On our way back we saw some wild animals!

After lunch we did a canoe tour on a beautiful lake. On the lake Sue and I put our feet in the water. When I tried to stand up in the canoe I almost fell out. Luckily Sue caught me! In the evening we made a camp-fire next to the cottage and grilled some sausages. I ate lots of them!
On Sunday morning we went on a bike trip.

We went to a market and I bought some cheese for my parents. Back at the cottage we had a snack, packed our things and got into the car. There was lots of traffic on the motorway. Sue and I were so tired that we slept for the whole drive.

It was a great weekend. We had so much fun! I really want to go to the Lake District again!

Fragen zum Text

31 Lies Tessas Tagebucheintrag und vervollständige die folgenden Sätze mit den unten angegebenen Satzenden.

a On Friday afternoon Tessa, Sue and Sue's parents …

____

b After dinner they played games and …

____

c It was a sunny Saturday morning so …

____

d After lunch they …

____

e When Tessa tried to stand up on the canoe …

____

f At the market …

____

g Tessa and Sue slept on the way home because …

____

… they watched a film.

… they arrived at the cottage.

… they went swimming.

… watched a film.

… they were so tired.

… she almost fell into the water.

… they hiked to the top of a mountain.

… did a canoe tour.

… talked for a long time.

… Tessa bought some cheese.

… she fell into the water.

… started their tour.

32 Tessa hat viele Fotos gemacht. Sie klebt sie in ihr Fotoalbum und beschriftet sie. Lies Tessas Tagebucheintrag noch einmal durch und schreibe die passenden Stellen aus ihrem Tagebuch unter die Fotos.

a

We played ______________________

____

b

____

____

c

____

____

d

____

____

e

____

____

f

____

____

Grammatik

Wann verwendest du das *simple past*?

Du verwendest das *simple past*, wenn du von in der **Vergangenheit abgeschlossenen Handlungen und Zuständen** berichten willst.

Beispiel: Last year, I visited my friends in London.
Letztes Jahr besuchte ich meine Freunde in London.

Weitere Signalwörter für das *simple past* sind z. B. *yesterday, last Monday/Tuesday/etc., in 1999* (oder ein anderes Jahr in der Vergangenheit).

Wie bildest du das *simple past* mit regelmäßigen Verben?

Die Form des *simple past* ist **für alle Personen gleich**. Du bildest sie folgendermaßen:
Grundform des Verbs (Infinitiv) + ***-ed***

1. Person Singular	I walked.	*Ich ging (zu Fuß).*
2. Person Singular	You walked.	*Du gingst (zu Fuß).*
3. Person Singular	He/she/it walked.	*Er/Sie/Es ging (zu Fuß).*
1. Person Plural	We walked.	*Wir gingen (zu Fuß).*
2. Person Plural	You walked.	*Ihr gingt (zu Fuß).*
3. Person Plural	They walked.	*Sie gingen (zu Fuß).*

Ausnahmen:

- An Verben, die auf ein stummes *-e* enden, hängst du nur *-d* an.
  Beispiel: like → liked
- Nach einem einzelnen, betonten Vokal verdoppelst du den Endkonsonanten und hängst *-ed* an.
  Beispiel: stop → stopped
- Endet ein Verb auf Konsonant + *-y*, so wandelst du das *y* in *i* + *-ed* um.
  Beispiel: carry → carried

33 Vervollständige folgende Tabelle mit den richtigen englischen Formen.

deutsche Grundform	englische Grundform	past tense
arbeiten	*work*	*worked*
reden		
öffnen		
helfen		
zu Fuß gehen		

deutsche Grundform	englische Grundform	past tense
spielen		
springen		
ansehen		
anrufen		

34 Nachdem Tessa ihrer Mutter von ihrem Aufenthalt erzählt hat, möchte Tessa wissen, was ihre Familie an dem Wochenende gemacht hat. Vervollständige die Erzählung mit den Verben aus Aufgabe 33. Verwende das *simple past.*

On Friday afternoon Dad ____________ in the garden and James ______________ him to cut the bushes. Later I ___________ to the shops to buy food for dinner. In the evening Dad and I ______________ the new film with Will Smith. It was really good. On Saturday morning I heard a strange noise. I ______________ the window and our neighbour's little black cat ____________ into the house. That was a surprise! James ____________ with it until lunch. In the early evening I ______________ your grandma. We ______________ for a long time. She's fine and wants you to visit her soon. Well, let's have dinner now.

Viele englische Verben haben eine **unregelmäßige Form** im *past tense.*
Unregelmäßige Verbformen musst du auswendig lernen.

Beispiele:	be – was/were	go – went	have – had
	do – did	make – made	say – said

Weitere unregelmäßige Verben findest du in einer Liste auf Seite 118.

Wie bildest du das *simple past* von *be*?

Das *simple past* von *be* hat zwei Formen: ***was*** (für *I, he, she, it*) und ***were*** (für alle anderen Personen).

1. Person Singular	I was in London.	*Ich war in London.*
2. Person Singular	You were in London.	*Du warst in London.*
3. Person Singular	He/She/It was in London.	*Er/Sie/Es war in London.*
1. Person Plural	We were in London.	*Wir waren in London.*
2. Person Plural	You were in London.	*Ihr wart in London.*
3. Person Plural	They were in London.	*Sie waren in London.*

35 Finde sechs unregelmäßige und drei regelmäßige Verben in Tessas Tagebucheintrag. Ergänze zu jedem Verb den Infinitiv.

unregelmäßige Verben	regelmäßige Verben
was / *be*	________ / ________
________ / ________	________ / ________
________ / ________	________ / ________
________ / ________	
________ / ________	
________ / ________	

36 Tessas Bruder James erzählt von seinem Wochenende. Vervollständige die Sätze und verwende das *simple past* der unregelmäßigen Verben in der Klammer.

Last Saturday ________ (be) great. My best friend Tom ________ (have) a birthday party in his garage. His parents ________ (give) him a big TV as a present. From his friends he ________ (get) some new DVDs. I ________ (buy) him a computer game. All the guests ________ (be) really nice. We ________ (eat) a lot of pizza and cake and ________ (drink) coke and lemonade. At midnight I ________ (go) home by bike.

Wortschatz

37 Tessa packt am Sonntagabend ihren Koffer *(suitcase)* aus. Sie hat einiges von ihrem Wochenend-Trip mitgebracht. Sieh dir die einzelnen Gegenstände an und vervollständige dann die Sätze mit den Namen der Gegenstände.

Tessa had a lovely weekend. She brought back some souvenirs from the Lake District: For her mum she picked a bunch of ____________________ from the meadow behind the cottage. At the market she bought some ____________________ for her dad, who loves to eat it with salty crackers and grapes. He also got a jar of strawberry ________________. Next to this present there are four ______________________________. Tessa got them from a farmer. The ____________________ in front of the suitcase are for James. They are from the lake Tessa and her friend swam in.

The weather was great and so Tessa needed her ____________________ and a pair of ______________________. Just before they started back home Tessa had found a beautiful duck's ______________________. She wants to glue it into her diary.

Schreiben

38 Was hast du vergangenes Wochenende gemacht und erlebt? Formuliere fünf Sätze auf Englisch und verwende das *simple past*. Nimm die Verben und Zeichnungen im Kalender zu Hilfe.

a On Friday evening I ______________________

____

b ______________________

____

c ______________________

____

d ______________________

____

e ______________________

____

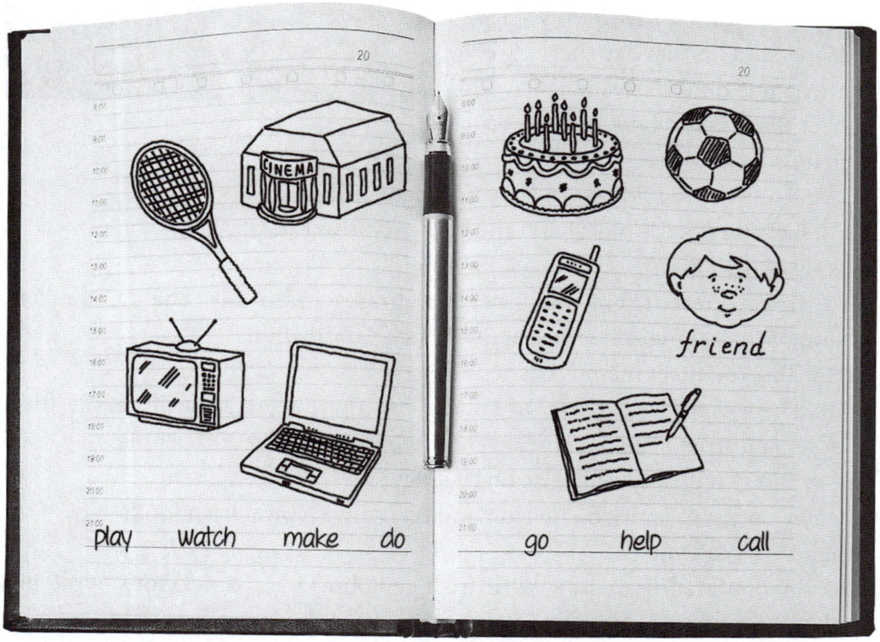

Topic 5: The exchange student

Tessa and her family are taking part in an exchange programme with the USA. Sean O'Sullivan, a pupil from Boston, is staying with the family for eight weeks. Last weekend he arrived in Greenwich. After dinner Sean showed some pictures of his family and life in America.

SEAN: That's a picture of last year's St. Patrick's Day Parade. My parents and I went to New York to watch the parade. Unfortunately, my brother didn't have time to go.

TESSA: What is St. Patrick's Day about?

SEAN: It's about St. Patrick, the patron saint *(Schutzheiliger)* of Ireland. He taught his religion to other people and founded *(gründete)* schools and churches.

TESSA: When is St. Patrick's Day?

SEAN: It is always on 17th March and on that day there are parades and festivals all over the world where Irish people live.

TESSA: And why did you go to New York to celebrate it?

SEAN: Because it's the oldest and the best parade in the USA.

TESSA: Did you like it?

SEAN: It was great! There were over 100 groups and bands. The parade went along 5th Avenue and ended at St. Patrick's Cathedral.

TESSA: Did you meet many Irish people?

SEAN: There were Irish there, of course, but there were a lot of people from other countries. The papers said there were about 700 000 people.

TESSA: Did you do anything else on that day?

SEAN: We went to an Irish Pub later and had some typical Irish food.

TESSA: What did you eat?

SEAN: We ordered Irish stew with Irish soda bread and a delicious apple pie. Maybe tomorrow I can show you how to make the bread.

TESSA: That would be great!

Fragen zum Text

39 Welche Bilder haben mit Seans Erzählung zu tun? Markiere sie (✓).

☐

☐

☐

☐

☐

40 Vervollständige den Text mithilfe von Seans Bericht.

St. Patrick is always on ____________________. It is said that Patrick died on that day in 461. People celebrate the fact that he brought his religion to Ireland and founded ______________ and ______________. Irish people all over the world have ____________________ on that day. The oldest parade is in ____________________. Lots of ________________ play music and you can eat ______________________ Irish food.

Grammatik

Wie verneinst du einen Satz im *simple past*?

Du verneinst einen Satz, indem du ***didn't (did not)* + Infinitiv** verwendest.

1. Person Singular	I didn't walk.	*Ich ging nicht (zu Fuß).*
2. Person Singular	You didn't walk.	*Du gingst nicht (zu Fuß).*
3. Person Singular	He/She/It didn't walk.	*Er/Sie/Es ging nicht (zu Fuß).*
1. Person Plural	We didn't walk.	*Wir gingen nicht (zu Fuß).*
2. Person Plural	You didn't walk.	*Ihr gingt nicht (zu Fuß).*
3. Person Plural	They didn't walk.	*Sie gingen nicht (zu Fuß).*

Möchtest du einen Satz verneinen, der eine Form von *to be* enthält, dann brauchst du **kein *did***, sondern du verneinst mit ***wasn't (was not)*** oder ***weren't (were not)***.

1. Person Singular	I wasn't there.	*Ich war nicht da.*
2. Person Singular	You weren't there.	*Du warst nicht da.*
3. Person Singular	He/She/It wasn't there.	*Er/Sie/Es war nicht da.*
1. Person Plural	We weren't there.	*Wir waren nicht da.*
2. Person Plural	You weren't there.	*Ihr wart nicht da.*
3. Person Plural	They weren't there.	*Sie waren nicht da.*

Auch wenn du ein Hilfsverb wie ***can*** im *simple past* verneinst, brauchst du kein *did*.

Beispiele:	I could swim.	I couldn't swim.	*Ich konnte nicht schwimmen.*
	He could swim.	He couldn't swim.	*Er konnte nicht schwimmen.*

41 Vervollständige die Sätze mit der verneinten *simple-past*-Form. Verwende dazu das jeweils passende Verb im Kasten.

get eat do play go ride

a I ______________________ my bike to school today.

b We ______________________ tickets for the concert.

c Dan ______________________ out with his friends last night.

d Matt ______________________ his history project.

e Lisa ______________________ much cake at the party.

f Theo ______________________ football with his friends because he was ill.

42 Schreibe die folgenden Sätze in der verneinten Form auf.

a We were in the city yesterday.

____

b The weather was great.

____

c There was a farmer's market on Saturday.

____

d My friends were too lazy to go shopping.

____

Wie bildest du Fragen und Kurzantworten im *simple past*?

- Wenn keine Form von *to be* und kein Hilfsverb vorhanden sind, bildest du **Fragesätze** immer mit ***did***. Auch hier muss das Verb im Infinitiv (ohne *to*) stehen.
  Beispiele: Did you like the party?
  Did he like the party?

  Die Satzstellung sieht folgendermaßen aus:
  ***Did* + Subjekt + Infinitiv + …**
  Beispiel: Did they go on holiday?
- Auf Fragen mit *did* kannst du **Kurzantworten** geben. Die Form *did(n't)* ist für alle Personen gleich.
  Beispiel: Did she ride the bike? No, she didn't.
  Yes, she did.

43 Beantworte die Fragen mit der richtigen Kurzantwort aus dem Kasten. Die Smileys helfen dir, die richtige Antwort zu finden.

– Yes, she did. – Yes, they did. – Yes, he did. – No, I didn't.
– No, you didn't. – No, it didn't. – Yes, we did.

a Did you visit the new car museum on Sunday? ☺

____

b Did I say we would meet at 4 o'clock? ☹

____

c Did Fred come on time? ☺

____

d Did you take out the rubbish? ☹

____

e Did Lina speak about the birthday present with you? ☺

____

f Did your brothers like the present? ☺

____

g Did the sun shine in Italy yesterday? ☹

____

44 Sean telefoniert mit seinen Eltern. Sie möchten wissen, wie er die erste Woche in England verbracht hat. Vervollständige die Fragen und beantworte sie mithilfe der Bilder.

a ____________ you meet Tessa's friends?
Yes, ______________.

b _______ Tessa go to school with you on the first day?

______________________________.

c _______ her parents show you around town?

______________________________.

d _______ you buy all your school books last week?

______________________________.

e ______________ you go to the tennis club?

______________________________________.

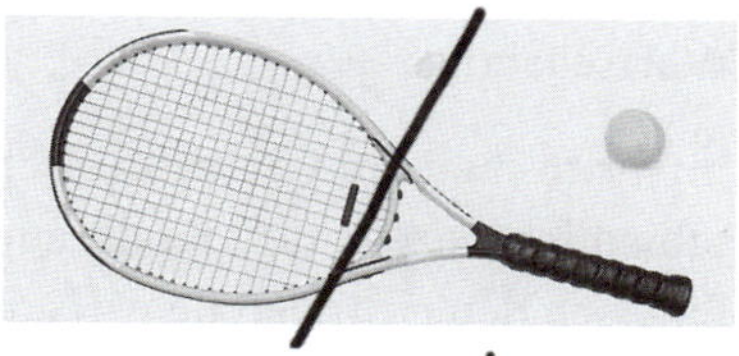

f ________ you miss us?

______________________________________.

Du kannst eine Frage im *simple past* auch mit einem **Fragewort** (*who, where, what, how, why, when*) beginnen.
Die Satzstellung sieht folgendermaßen aus:

Fragewort + *did* + Subjekt + Infinitiv + …

Beispiel: What did you do yesterday?

Beachte: Wenn du das Fragewort ***who*** in der Bedeutung ‚**wer**' verwendest, verwendest du *did* nicht.

Beispiel: Who went to London? Jane went to London.
Wer fuhr nach London? Jane fuhr nach London.

45 Vervollständige die Fragen mit einem passenden Fragewort.

a ________________ you go to school? – I went to St. Patrick's School.

b ________________ you meet in town? – I met my best friend and her sister.

c ______________ you eat for breakfast? – I ate toast and jam.

d ________________ you like the game? – It was interesting!

e ______________ you leave the house? – We left the house at 7.40 a.m.

f ______________________ she call me? – She didn't call you because she didn't have time.

Wortschatz

46 Im britischen und amerikanischen Englisch werden viele Dinge oft unterschiedlich bezeichnet. Finde zur jeweiligen Bezeichnung aus dem britischen Englisch den richtigen Begriff aus dem amerikanischen Englisch.

soccer sneakers fall
apartment candy chips
cookie elevator

biscuits		
crisps		
football		
sweets		

flat

autumn

lift

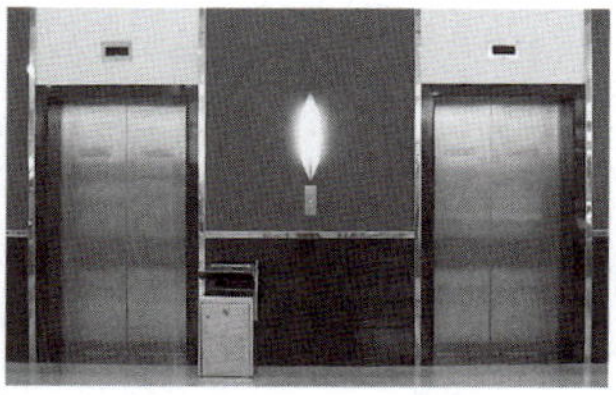

trainers

47 Welche Gegenstände von oben werden hier beschrieben? Verwende jeweils die amerikanische Bezeichnung.

a They are made of potatoes. ____________________

b It's a popular sport in Germany. ____________________

c They are in all tall buildings. ____________________

d Halloween and Thanksgiving are in this season. ____________________

e It's a place to live in. ____________________

Schreiben

48 Zurück in den USA trifft Sean sich mit seinen Freunden. Welche Fragen wurden ihm gestellt und was hat er geantwortet? Schreibe die Sätze auf Englisch, ohne die deutschen Sätze direkt zu übersetzen. Sie dir das Beispiel an.

JOHN: Did you like it in England? ______

John fragt, ob es Sean in England gefallen hat.

SEAN: ______

Sean sagt, dass es ihm sehr gefallen hat.

LISA: ______

Lisa fragt, ob er Tessas Freunde kennengelernt hat.

SEAN: ______

Ja, er hat sie getroffen und fand sie sehr nett.

JOHN: ______

John fragt, ob sie auf einer Party waren.

SEAN: ______

Nein, sie waren nicht auf einer Party. Sie sind auf ein Popkonzert gegangen.

DAVID: ______

David fragt, ob Sean auch Sport gemacht hat.

SEAN: ______

Ja, er hat Hockey gespielt.

LISA: ______

Lisa fragt, wann die Schule immer angefangen hat.

SEAN: ______

Sean sagt, dass sie immer um 9 Uhr angefangen hat.

JOHN: ______

John fragt, ob Sean Amerika vermisst hat.

SEAN: ______

Sean sagt, dass er oft an zu Hause gedacht hat.

Topic 6: A date on Valentine's Day

It's Valentine's Day next week. Two boys from school want to go out with Tessa, but she doesn't know who she wants to date. She asks Sue for help.

Jonathan is really good-looking and the nicest boy at school. He is 13 years old and lives next door. We sometimes walk to school together. He has short, black hair and is taller than me. Jonathan has got two younger sisters.
He is the best football player in the school team. He trains four times a week. He is not as good at Maths as he is as at sports.
Jonathan likes Italian food just like me. He cooks for his family once a week.

Eric is cool. He likes trendy clothes and we both love hip hop. He is 12 years old. He has got an older brother.
Eric's hair is brown and longer than Jonathan's hair. Eric is shorter than Jonathan. He isn't a sports fan, but he loves music. Eric listens to all sorts of music and also plays the guitar. He is better at Maths than Jonathan.
Eric is the funniest boy at school. He loves to tell jokes and always makes me smile.

Fragen zum Text

49 Sue fasst Tessas Informationen über die beiden Jungen zusammen. Hat sie sich alles richtig gemerkt? Hake (✓) ab, ob ihre Aussagen richtig *(true)*, falsch *(false)* oder nicht im Text *(not in the text)* sind.

	true	false	not in the text
a Jonathan is the funniest boy at school.	☐	☐	☐
b Jonathan is younger than Eric.	☐	☐	☐
c Tessa is Jonathan's neighbour.	☐	☐	☐
d Jonathan has got two younger brothers.	☐	☐	☐
e Eric and Jonathan are friends.	☐	☐	☐
f Jonathan is good at sports.	☐	☐	☐
g Eric's hair is shorter than Jonathan's hair.	☐	☐	☐
h Eric is shorter than Jonathan.	☐	☐	☐
i Tessa and Eric like the same food.	☐	☐	☐
j Eric likes music better than sports.	☐	☐	☐

50 Ordne durch Verbindungslinien die richtigen Eigenschaften und Hobbys dem jeweiligen Jungen zu. Ein Bild passt zu keinem der beiden Jungen.

Grammatik

Was sind Adjektive?

Adjektive (Wiewörter) beschreiben die **Eigenschaften** oder **Merkmale** eines Nomens (Namenwortes) näher.

- Adjektive können **vor einem Nomen** stehen.
  Beispiel: I would like to have a fast bike. *Ich möchte ein schnelles Fahrrad haben.*
- Adjektive können auch nach bestimmten Verben stehen, v. a. **nach** einer **Form von** ***be***.
  Beispiel: My bike is fast. *Mein Fahrrad ist schnell.*

Adjektive können gesteigert werden und es können Vergleiche angestellt werden.

Wie bildest du die Steigerungsformen der Adjektive?

- **Adjektive mit ein oder zwei Silben** werden folgendermaßen gesteigert:
  Beispiel: long – longer – (the) longest *lang – länger – am längsten*
  Du hängst ***-er*** an, wenn du zwei Personen oder Dinge vergleichst.
  Wenn du mindestens drei Personen oder Dinge vergleichst, hängst du ***-est*** an.

  Beachte:
  Bei einsilbigen Adjektiven mit **Vokal + Konsonant** musst du den Konsonanten am Ende verdoppeln und *-er* oder *-est* anhängen:
  Beispiel: big – bigger – (the) biggest

  Endet das **Adjektiv auf** ***-e***, hängst du nur *-r* oder *-st* an:
  Beispiel: large – larger – (the) largest

  Bei **zweisilbigen Adjektiven auf** ***-y*** wird bei der Steigerung das *-y* zu *-i*:
  Beispiel: happy – happier – (the) happiest

51 Trage die fehlenden Formen der Adjektive in die Tabelle ein.

Grundform des Adjektivs	1. Steigerungsstufe	2. Steigerungsstufe
cheap		
		the hardest
hot		
		the oldest
nice		
dry	drier	
		the busiest

- **Zweisilbige Adjektive, die nicht auf *-le*, *-er*, *-y* und *-ow* enden**, sowie **mehrsilbige Adjektive** steigerst du, indem du dem Adjektiv ***more*** oder ***most*** voranstellst.
  Beispiele: stupid – more stupid – (the) most stupid
  difficult – more difficult – (the) most difficult

52 Trage die fehlenden Formen der Adjektive in die Tabelle ein.

expensive		
important		
		the most interesting

Es gibt auch **unregelmäßige Steigerungsformen**. Diese musst du dir merken.

Beispiele:
bad – worse – (the) worst — *schlecht – schlechter – am schlechtesten*
good – better – (the) best — *gut – besser – am besten*
a lot of/many/much – more – (the) most — *viel – mehr – am meisten*

53 Vervollständige die Sätze mit der richtigen Steigerungsform der unterstrichenen Adjektive.

a Bob is strong but Timothy is ______________________.
Clive is the ____________________________.

b My new trainers were cheap but Alan's new shoes were ______________.
Ann's sandals were ____________________________.

c Did Joey get many presents for Christmas? Yes, he did. But Samuel got
______________ and Lily got ________________________________.

d Susie's cocoa is hot. Dan's cocoa is _________________.
Olivia's tea is ___________________________.

e Lisa's hair is short but Peter's hair is _________________.
Peter's brother has got ________________ hair.

f Our house is old but Grandma's house is _________________. My aunt's
house is ___________________________.

g Simon's shirts are <u>dirty</u>. The white shirt is the ______________________.

h Ruth has got three <u>younger</u> brothers. Finn is ____________________.

i Rome and Paris are <u>big</u> cities in Europe, but London is ________________ and Moscow is ______________ city in Europe.

j I'm <u>good</u> at Biology, but I'm ______________ at Geography. I'm ______________ at Maths.

k Mr Tuck's rubbish smells really <u>bad</u>. Mrs Taylor thinks her bin smells ______________ and Mr Todd's rubbish smells ________________.

54 Setze die richtige Steigerungsform der Adjektive auf Englisch in die Lücken ein.

a I think volleyball is boring. Football is ___________________________ *(spannend)*.

b The _________________________________ *(langweilig)* sport is golf.

c The Beatles are the ____________________________ *(berühmt)* pop band of all times.

d I think sharks are the _________________________________ *(gefährlich)* animals in the sea.

e The flat isn't cheap, but the house is ______________________________ *(teuer)*.

Wie bildest du Vergleiche und wann stellst du sie an?

Du gebrauchst Vergleiche, wenn du Gleichheit oder Ungleichheit zwischen Personen oder Dingen ausdrücken willst.

Du kannst **zwei unterschiedliche Dinge oder Personen** folgendermaßen miteinander **vergleichen**:

1. Steigerungsstufe des Adjektivs + *than*

Beispiel: Tom's car is <u>bigger</u> <u>than</u> Simon's car.
Toms Auto ist größer als Simons Auto.

Tom's car is <u>more</u> <u>expensive</u> <u>than</u> Simon's car.
Toms Auto ist teurer als Simons Auto.

55 Tessa und ihr Verehrer überlegen, zu welcher Veranstaltung sie am Valentinstag gehen sollen. Lies dir die Flyer gut durch.

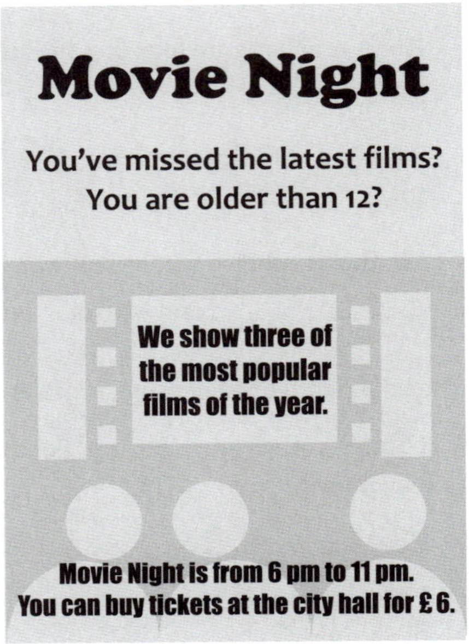

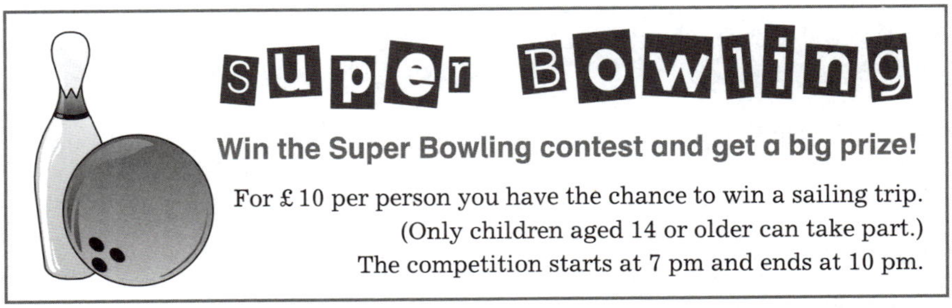

Stelle nun Vergleiche mit *than* an. Verwende die Adjektive *cheap, long, old, early* und *late* je einmal.

a A ticket for Movie Night is ______________________ a ticket for the Super Bowling.

b Movie Night ends ______________________ the Super Bowling.

c The School Concert takes ______________________ the Super Bowling.

d For the Super Bowling you have to be ______________________ for the School Concert.

e Movie Night starts ______________________ the Super Bowling.

Wortschatz

56 Kennst du die gesuchten Gegensätze oder Paare?

a

small	–	______	left	–	______
mother	–	______	daughter	–	______
black	–	______	warm	–	______
bitter	–	______	upstairs	–	______
slowly	–	______	dirty	–	______
come	–	______	poor	–	______
day	–	______	hello	–	______

b Ergänze nun die Reime mit passenden Wörtern aus der obigen Aufgabe.

People can be tall or ______.
They all live on a big round ball.

Some people are very old,
the weather can be warm or ______.

There was a big fight
in the street last ______.

I have to ______
and leave the show.

The moon and stars are in the sky,
don't forget to say ______.

Schreiben

57 Tessa hat sich entschieden, mit Eric auszugehen. Schwärmend berichtet Eric seinem Freund Ben von der Verabredung.
Vervollständige seine E-Mail und benutze gegebenenfalls nebenstehende Begriffe.

Topic 7: A birthday surprise

It's Tessa's birthday tomorrow. Her mum, dad and her brother James want to surprise her with a party. Now they are in town to do some shopping.

MUM: James, have a look at the guest list. How many people are on it?

JAMES: It's 10 friends and us.

DAD: OK, so let's buy some drinks first. We haven't got much coke at home. How much is it?

MUM: It's £ 7.20 for six bottles. Let's take them and some bottles of lemonade. We've got lots of juice at home.

JAMES: What about hot dogs?

MUM: That's a good idea. How many sausages and rolls do we need to make them?

DAD: I think 25 sausages and rolls are enough. Look, they've got a lot of different sorts of sausages. James, you can choose.

JAMES: Can we get sweets and crisps, too?

MUM: Yes, you go and find out how much they are. I'll look for some chocolate ice-cream.

DAD: We still need lots of candles and balloons. I'll get them.

JAMES: Wait! Here are the sweets. They only cost 99 p!

MUM: Those are definitely too many sweets! Put half of them back, please. We don't want to spend much money on sweets.

DAD: How much time have we got until Tessa comes back home?

MUM: Not much! Tessa will be back in about two hours.

DAD: So hurry up! I'll meet you and James at the checkout.

Fragen zum Text

58 Was hat die Familie im Supermarkt gekauft? Vervollständige die Einkaufsliste.

59 Füge in die Sprechblasen die passende Stelle aus dem Text ein.

a

b

c

d

e

f

Grammatik

Wie drückst du eine unbestimmte Anzahl oder Menge im Englischen aus?
Manchmal willst du die genaue Zahl nicht sagen. Solche unbestimmten Mengenangaben kannst du mit ***a lot of***, ***lots of***, ***much*** und ***many*** machen.

Wann verwendest du *a lot of* und *lots of*?
A lot of und *lots of* bedeuten ‚viele' oder ‚viel'. Du verwendest sie hauptsächlich in **bejahten Aussagesätzen** und kannst sie dort beliebig miteinander austauschen.
Beispiel: There are a lot of / lots of cars on the road.
Auf der Straße sind viele Autos.

60 Bringe die Satzteile in die richtige Reihenfolge und füge dann *a lot of* oder *lots of* an der richtigen Stelle ein.

a for the party / things / buys / Tessa's family
Tessa's family buys a lot of/lots of things for the party.

b on her birthday / Tessa / presents / gets

____

c There / in the supermarket / are / people

____

d buy / sweets / You / in the shop / can

____

e will come / Tessa's friends / to the party

____

Wann verwendest du *many* und wann verwendest du *much*?

- *Many* bedeutet ‚viele'. Du verwendest es, wenn etwas **gezählt** werden kann.
  Beispiele: a hundred men → many men *viele Männer*
- *Much* bedeutet ‚viel'. Du verwendest es, wenn etwas **nicht gezählt** werden kann und du z. B. nicht „zwei …, drei …" sagen kannst.
  Diese Nomen haben keine Pluralform.
  Beispiele: cream → much cream *viel Sahne*
  rain → much rain *viel Regen*

61 Suche aus dem Lesetext jeweils vier Nomen heraus, die in Verbindung mit *much* oder *many* stehen.

much	many

62 Welche Begriffe sind hier abgebildet? Schreibe die englischen Wörter zusammen mit *many* oder *much* unter das jeweilige Bild.

a
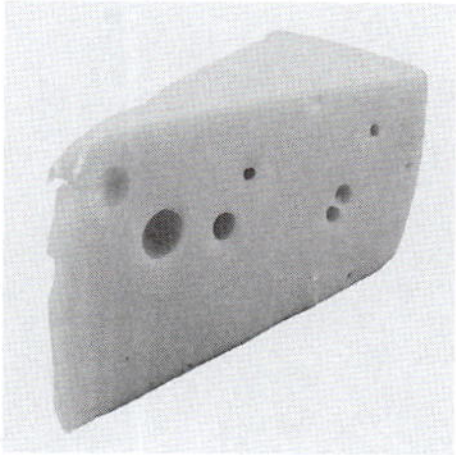

b

c

d

e

f

g

h

i

In welcher Art von Sätzen verwendest du *many* und *much*?

- Du verwendest *much* und *many* mit den Wörtern ***too*** und ***so***.
  Beispiele: Don't eat so much cake!
  Iss nicht so viel Kuchen!
  There are too many cars on the roads.
  Es gibt zu viele Autos auf den Straßen.
- Du verwendest *much* und *many* normalerweise in **verneinten Sätzen** und in **Fragen**.
  Beispiele: Peter doesn't have much money. *Peter hat nicht viel Geld.*
  Have you got many books? *Hast du viele Bücher?*

63 Vervollständige folgende Sätze mit *much, many* oder *lots of/a lot of.*

a There are __________ guests in the room.

b Tessa's parents didn't buy too __________ lemonade.

c How __________ candles are on the cake?

d I got so __________ presents! Thank you!

e How __________ CDs have we got?

f Did Tessa's mother make __________ cakes for the party?

g There are __________ boys and girls from Tessa's class at the party.

h How __________ money did you get?

i __________ guests have to go home early.

j There isn't __________ coke left at the end of the party.

Wortschatz

64 Hier siehst du ein Bild von Tessas Party. Schreibe die englischen Bezeichnungen der Gegenstände unter das Bild neben die Zahlen. Füge noch mindestens drei weitere Sachen hinzu, die du ebenfalls auf Englisch beschriftest.

1 ______________________	7 ______________________
2 ______________________	8 ______________________
3 ______________________	9 ______________________
4 ______________________	10 ______________________
5 ______________________	11 ______________________
6 ______________________	12 ______________________

65 Welche Lebensmittel und Getränke werden hier gesucht? Ergänze die fehlenden Vokale (a, e, i, o, u).

str _ wb _ rry / _ ppl _ / p _ t _ t _ _ s / t _ _ / j _ m / p _ st _

s _ l _ d / fr _ _ t / b _ _ ns / ch _ ck _ n / f _ sh / m _ lk

Setze nun die passenden Wörter in die folgenden Sätze ein:

a I love to eat ____________________ ice-cream.

b Susy eats her cornflakes with lots of ________________.

c An _________________ a day keeps the doctor away.

d My mother puts sugar and milk in her _________________.

e For breakfast Julian wants to have bread and butter and _______________.

f The Italians are famous for their delicious ________________.

g Chips are made from _________________.

Schreiben

66 Du möchtest deinen Geburtstag mit deinen Freunden feiern. Schreibe ihnen eine Einladung, die folgende Punkte beinhaltet: Anrede, Grund der Feier, Datum, Ort, Uhrzeit, Rückmeldung per Anruf/E-Mail, Verabschiedung

Topic 8: What's next?

In the classroom there is a big calendar on the wall. Pupils from Year 8 write down their birthdays, class tests and school events. Here's one month of the calendar.

JUNE						
1	2 start writing book report	3	4	5 Steve (12)	6	7
8 Eric (12)	9	10 book report presentation	11	12 school concert	13	14
15	16	17	18	19 History test	20	21
22 Zoe (13)	23	24	25 sports day	26	27	28
29 holiday!	30 holiday!					

Fragen zum Text

67 Sieh dir den Kalender an und beantworte dann die Fragen auf Englisch. Schreibe in ganzen Sätzen.

a What's on 12th June?

____

b Whose birthday is first in the month of June?

____

c What is two weeks after Eric's birthday?

____

d How much time do the pupils have to write the book report?

____

e How many days is Steve older than Eric?

____

f Why are the pupils happy on the last days of June?

____

68 Es müssen neue Termine in den Kalender eingetragen werden. Welche Daten gibt der Lehrer bekannt? Notiere jeweils passende Stichwörter an der richtigen Stelle im Kalender.

"The Maths exam is on the ninth in the first lesson."

"The trip to the National Museum is on the fifteenth."

"There's no school on the day before the History test."

"The Internet workshop is on the first of June."

Grammatik

Was sind Ordnungszahlen?

Mit **Ordnungszahlen** gibst du eine **bestimmte Reihenfolge** an. Eine Ordnungszahl antwortet also auf die Frage **„der/die/das wievielte?"**.
Ordnungszahlen werden gebildet, indem man *-th* an die Grundzahl hängt. Ausnahmen sind *first, second* und *third*.
Beispiel: This is the fourth time you're late. *Du bist zum vierten Mal zu spät.*

Ordnungszahlen bis 30:

1st	first	11th	eleventh	21st	twenty-first
2nd	second	12th	twelfth	22nd	twenty-second
3rd	third	13th	thirteenth	23rd	twenty-third
4th	fourth	14th	fourteenth	24th	twenty-fourth
5th	fifth	15th	fifteenth	25th	twenty-fifth
6th	sixth	16th	sixteenth	26th	twenty-sixth
7th	seventh	17th	seventeenth	27th	twenty-seventh
8th	eighth	18th	eighteenth	28th	twenty-eighth
9th	ninth	19th	nineteenth	29th	twenty-ninth
10th	tenth	20th	twentieth	30th	thirtieth
				…	

Merke: Im Deutschen steht nach der Ordnungszahl ein **Punkt**, im Englischen stehen die **beiden letzten Buchstaben** der Ordnungszahl.
Beispiel: 2nd *(englische Schreibweise)* 2. *(deutsche Schreibweise)*

69 Heute ist Sporttag an der Schule. John gibt die Ergebnisse des Hockeywettbewerbs bekannt. Sieh dir seine Notizen an und fülle die Lücken aus.

The Blue Eyes are in ________________ place.
They won every match!
The ________________ best team is *Nightmare*.
The Lucky Six are in ________________ place.
Goals 4U are in ________________ place,
The Elephants came ________________,
The Chatterboxes came ________________
and *The Socks* are in ________________ place.
They didn't win any match.
Congratulations to the winning team!

70 Male die gesuchten Smileys in der jeweiligen Reihe an. Wenn du alle gefunden hast, entsteht ein Bild. Welcher Buchstabe ist es?

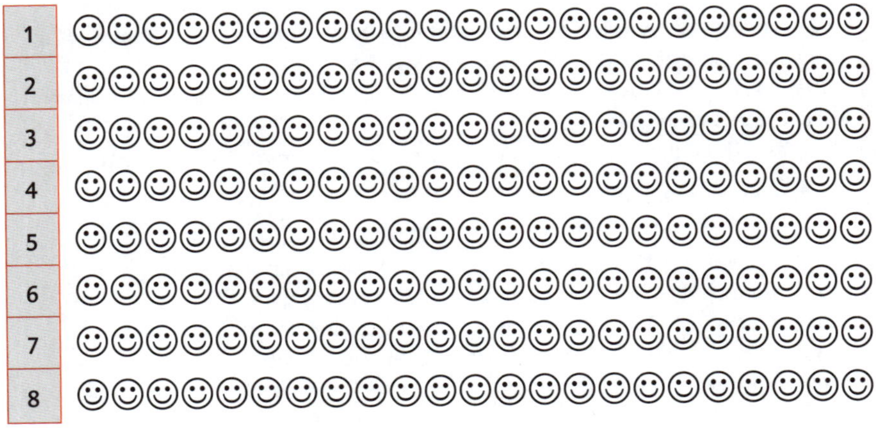

	smiley number
1	second, twenty-second
2	third, twenty-first
3	forth, twentieth
4	fifth, nineteenth
5	sixth, twelfth, eighteenth
6	seventh, eleventh, thirteenth, seventeenth
7	eighth, tenth, fourteenth, sixteenth
8	ninth, fifteenth

Finde fünf Wörter, die mit diesem Buchstaben beginnen:

a ______________________________

b ______________________________

c ______________________________

d ______________________________

e ______________________________

Wie schreibst du auf Englisch das Datum und wie sprichst du es aus?
Im britischen Englisch kannst du das Datum folgendermaßen schreiben und aussprechen:

		Tag		**Monat**	**Jahr**
Schreibweise:		1st		April	2012
		1		April	2012
Aussprache:	*the*	*first*	*of*	*April*	2012
oder:		**Monat**		**Tag**	**Jahr**
Schreibweise		April		1st	2012
Aussprache		*April*		*the first*	2012

Um ein Datum anzugeben, verwendest du folgende **Präpositionen**:
Beispiele: He was born **in** 1998.
He was born **in** July 1998.
He was born **on** 14th July 1998.

71 Ordne die Kinder den Geburtsdaten zu und schreibe den angegebenen Buchstaben in das jeweils richtige Kästchen. Die Buchstaben ergeben in der richtigen Reihenfolge ein Wort.

- Hannah's birthday is on the nineteenth of August. (E)
- Eric's birthday is on the thirteenth of December. (I)
- Ali's birthday is on the eleventh of April. (U)
- George was born on the twenty-first of January. (P)
- Sarah's birthday is on the ninth of April. (S)
- Sue was born on the first of May. (R)
- Theo's birthday is on the eighteenth of March. (R)
- Sylvie was born on the second of January. (S)

9th April	23rd Jan	11th April	18th Dec	1st May	21st Jan	5th Jan

18th Mar	21st Aug	13th Dec	2nd Jan	9th Mar	19th Aug

birthday ____________________

Wortschatz

72 Monate, Wochentage, Ordnungszahlen: Welches Wort fehlt in der Reihe?

a November, December, ____________________, February

b nineteenth, twentieth, ______________________, twenty-second

c Sunday, Monday, Tuesday, ____________________

d second, third, fourth, ____________________

e Wednesday, Thursday, ____________________, Saturday

f March, April, ____________________, June

73 Ordne die Wetterbegriffe den Bildern zu und schreibe sie in die Kästchen.

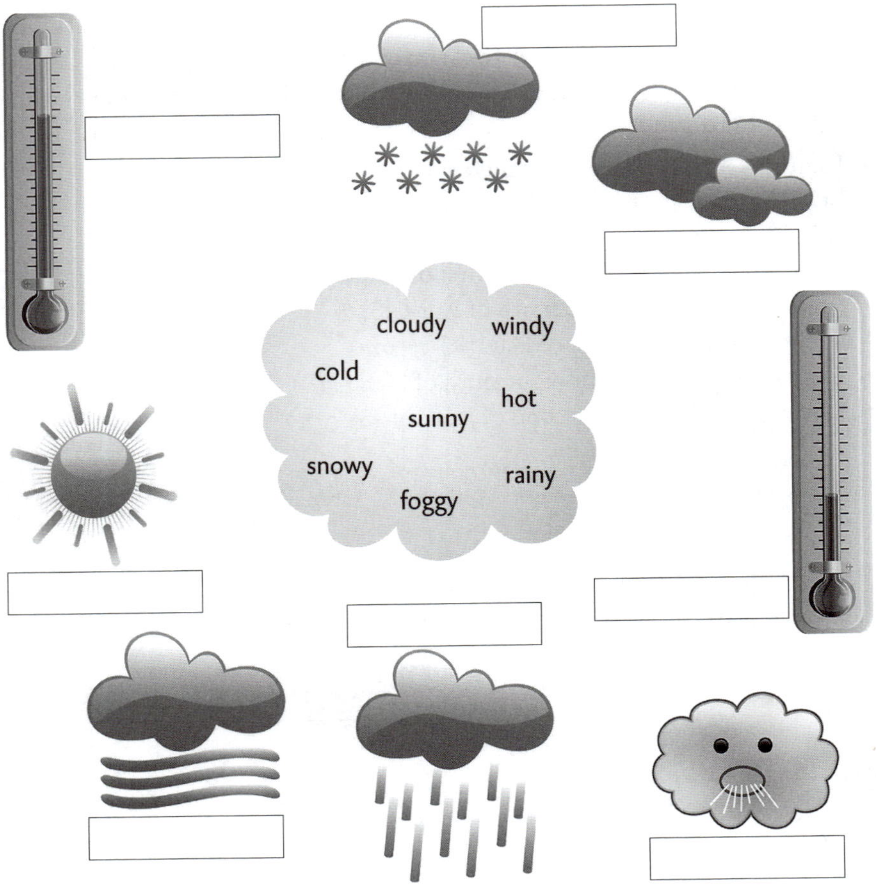

Schreiben

74 Du schreibst deinem englischen Freund Nick von dem Talentwettbewerb an deiner Schule. Verwende die Notizen, um ganze Sätze zu schreiben. Versuche auch, Sätze mit den Adjektiven zu bilden.

good	~~fantastic~~
exciting	nice
interesting	clever

1. Lisa: sang "My heart will go on."
2. Itsy the dog: did tricks
3. Kevin: danced like Justin Timberlake
4. Tim and Peter: music – with glasses

Hi Nick,

Yesterday was the talent show at my school. It was so much fun. The top four were great. In first place was ____________. She ______________________

____. It was fantastic!

In ____

____

____

____

____

____

____

____

____

____

____

____

____

____

____

And how was your week?

Topic 9: The website

School website

- Home
- About us
- Gallery
- Teachers
- What's on this term
- Library
- A – Z listings
- Downloads
- Contact us

The talent show

In the last week of April our school organised a talent show.
20 pupils aged between 12 and 16 showed the jury their best talent. Our art, music and P. E. teachers were the jury. Lots of pupils didn't want to miss this event and supported their favourite acts. Most of them were singing acts, of course. Boys and girls sang famous songs from the charts, but there were also great hip hop dances.
The winner of our talent show wasn't a pupil. Max, a boy from Year 8, brought his parrot, "Cheeky", who could count, sing, dance and do acrobatic tricks. The jury decided that he was the winner of the show. Congratulations!

More pictures of the talent show can be found in the gallery.

Fragen zum Text

75 Besucher der Homepage möchten der Seite verschiedene Informationen entnehmen. Schreibe auf, welche Rubrik sie anklicken müssen.

a Mrs Tompson wants to know the school's address.

b Mr Eden is looking for a new school for his daughter. He wants some information about the school's profile.

c Greg wants to borrow a book.

d Adam wants to see some pictures of the talent show.

e Mr Cain has to call his son's Maths teacher.

f Sue lost her form for the Internet project. She needs a new one.

76 Ein Schüler hat den Text "The talent show" verfasst und seiner Lehrerin zum Korrigieren gegeben, bevor er ins Internet gestellt wurde. Vergleiche ihn mit dem Text auf Seite 72, streiche die Fehler durch und schreibe sie verbessert auf die Linie. Beachte: nicht in jedem Satz verbirgt sich ein Fehler.

The talent show

In the last week of April our school organisd a talent show.

20 pupils aged betwen 12 and 16 showed the jury there best talent.

Lots of people didn't want to miss this event and supported they're favourite acts.

Most of them were famous acts, of course.

Boys and girls sang famous songs from the charts,

but there were also great hip hop dances.

The winner of our show weren't a pupil.

Max, a boy from Year 8, took his parrot "Cheeky", which could count, sing, dance and do acrobatic tricks. ______________________

The jury decided that he was the winner of the show. ______________________

Congratulations! ______________________

77 In dem Bericht kommt das Wort *of* häufig vor. Suche die entsprechenden Stellen aus dem Text heraus und schreibe sie wie im Beispiel auf. Übersetze sie anschließend ins Deutsche.

English	**German**
last week of April	______________________
______________________	______________________
______________________	______________________
______________________	______________________
______________________	______________________

Grammatik

Wann verwendest du den *of*-Genitiv?

Mit dem Genitiv zeigt man Besitz oder Zugehörigkeit an. Du kennst bereits den s-Genitiv, der nur für Personen verwendet wird:

Beispiel: Mary's house — *Marys Haus.*

Den *of*-Genitiv verwendet man dagegen nur **bei Dingen:**

Beispiel: the colour of the house — *die Farbe des Hauses*

Wie bildest du den *of*-Genitiv?

Du bildest den *of*-Genitiv, indem du **vor das Nomen, das im Genitiv stehen soll, *of the*** oder ***of a (an)*** stellst.

Beispiele: the end of the line — *das Ende der (Warte-)Schlange*

the start of a new year — *der Anfang eines neuen Jahres*

78 Bilde aus den folgenden Wörtern jeweils einen Satz mit dem *of*-Genitiv.

a last letter – alphabet – 'z'

The last letter of the alphabet is 'z'.

b first day – week – Monday

____

c name – Bavarian city – Munich

____

d winner – game – Peter

____

e colour – sofa – green

____

f title – song – "Back Home"

____

Wann wird die *of*-Form noch verwendet?

- Bei feststehenden Ausdrücken wie ***a lot of*** bzw. ***lots of***:
  Beispiele: I always drink a lot of / lots of water. — *Ich trinke immer viel Wasser.*
  A lot of / Lots of people learn English. — *Viele Leute lernen Englisch.*
- **Bei Behältnissen** musst du im Englischen immer ***of*** hinzufügen. Im Deutschen übersetzt du of nicht.
  Beispiele: a bottle of water — *eine Flasche Wasser*
  glass of orange juice — *ein Glas Orangensaft*

79 Setze die Angaben in die Lücken ein, sodass ein sinnvoller Satz entsteht.

a lot of	glass of	cup of	bag of	spoon of	bowl of	plate of	bottle of

a My parents often drink a ______________ tea for breakfast.

b Fred is thirsty. He needs a big ______________ water.

c Mum cut up apples, strawberries and melons this morning.
Now there is a ______________ fruit in the fridge.

d I don't like black coffee. I put a ______________ sugar in the cup.

e Angela went shopping. She went home with a ____________________ clothes.

f Chris isn't hungry any more. He ate a ____________________ steak and fries.

g Can I have a ____________________ coke, please?

h There are ____________________ children in our neighbourhood.

Wortschatz

80 Im Schulorchester spielen die Schüler unterschiedliche Instrumente. Hier siehst du ein paar Schüler beim Proben. Welche Instrumente spielen sie? Ergänze die jeweiligen Wörter mit den richtigen Buchstaben. Ein Instrument ist auf den Bildern jedoch nicht zu sehen.

t__u__ __et d__u__s

v__o__in g__it__r

ce__ __o f__ut__

sa__op__o__e p__a__o

Schreiben

81 Zum Thema „Musik“ sollt ihr eure Mitschüler über ihren Musikgeschmack befragen. Beantworte die Fragen eines Klassenkameraden mit vollständigen Sätzen.

a What kind of music do you like?

____

____

b Who is your favourite singer?

____

____

c What band do you like best?

____

d What is your favourite song?

____

____

e When do you listen to music?

____

____

f What music do your parents like?

____

____

Topic 10: Packing a bag

James and his best friend Dan are going to Portsmouth on the south coast of England. They are going to spend the weekend at a beach volleyball camp. James' mum checks his bag:

Mum: Let's see. Do you have any socks in your bag?

James: Yes, I have some socks in there and my trainers.

Mum: What about T-shirts and shorts? Do you have enough?

James: I think so. There are four T-shirts and two pairs of shorts.

Mum: Do you have any sun cream and your swimming trunks?

James: I don't have any sun cream. I'll buy some in Portsmouth. I took my green and my blue swimming trunks.

Mum: That's fine. Do you have any clothes for the evenings when it's cold?

James: I have two pullovers, my new pair of trousers and a jacket. Can you give me some sweets for the trip?

Mum: Yes, I can. I'll give you some chocolate later.

James: Great! And don't forget something to drink.

Mum: Of course not. Is there any shampoo, toothpaste and a toothbrush in your bag? And your glasses? Don't forget to wear them!

James: Yep, it's all in there.

Mum: Is there anything else I can give you?

James: Nope. I'm done, thanks.

Mum: I know what you still don't have – a picture of your lovely mum!

James: That's not funny, mum! I'm not a baby any more!

Fragen zum Text

82 Welche dieser Gegenstände hat James schon eingepackt? Kreuze die richtigen Bilder an.

☐

☐

☐

☐

☐

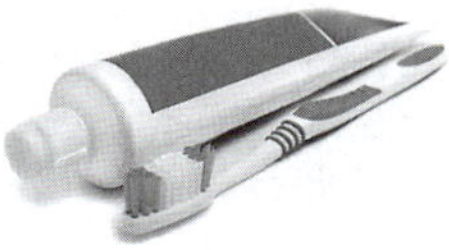
☐

☐

☐

☐

83 Nenne sechs weitere Dinge auf Englisch, die schon in der Tasche sind.

a ______________________ **b** ______________________

c ______________________ **d** ______________________

e ______________________ **f** ______________________

Grammatik

Wann verwendest du *some* und *any*?

Im Englischen drückt man mit *some* und *any* eine **unbestimmte Anzahl oder Menge** aus (einige, etwas, ein paar). Im Deutschen werden *some* und *any* oft nicht übersetzt.

Wann verwendest du ***some***?

- *Some* verwendest du meist bei **bejahten Aussagen:**
  Beispiel: There are some books on the table.
  Es liegen ein paar/einige Bücher auf dem Tisch.
- bei **Bitten:**
  Beispiel: Could I have some water, please?
  Könnte ich bitte (etwas) Wasser haben?
- oder bei **Angeboten:**
  Beispiel: Would you like some lemonade?
  Hättest du gerne (etwas) Limonade?

Wann verwendest du ***any***?

- *Any* verwendest du meist bei **verneinten Aussagen:**
  Beispiel: There aren't any books on the table.
  Es liegen keine Bücher auf dem Tisch.
- und bei **Fragen:**
  Beispiel: Is there any chocolate left?
  Ist noch (etwas) Schokolade übrig?

84 Setze in jeden Satz *some* oder *any* an die richtige Stelle. Schreibe den Satz noch einmal auf und übersetze ihn dann.

a Mike meets friends in front of the cinema.

____

____

b Would you like chocolate?

____

____

c Could you give me salt for my egg, please?

____

____

d There isn't water in the fridge.

e I don't have salami, but I can give you cheese.

Wann verwendest du *somebody/something* und *anybody/anything?*

Die Regel für *some* und *any* gilt auch für ihre Zusammensetzungen:

- *somebody* (jemand) und *something* (etwas): bei bejahten Aussagen, Bitten oder Angeboten

  Beispiele: Somebody is in the house. — *Jemand ist im Haus.*

  I would like to eat something. — *Ich möchte gerne etwas essen.*

- *anybody* und *anything:* bei Fragen und verneinten Aussagen

  Beispiele: There isn't anybody in the house. — *Niemand ist im Haus.*

  Would you like anything else? — *Möchtest du noch etwas?*

85 Ordne die folgenden Sätze dem jeweils richtigen Bild zu. Ein Bild passt nicht.

(A) "Can somebody help me, please?"
(B) "Is it anybody's birthday?"
(C) "Look, there is something on the table."
(D) "There isn't anything on the table."
(E) "Can I have something to drink?"

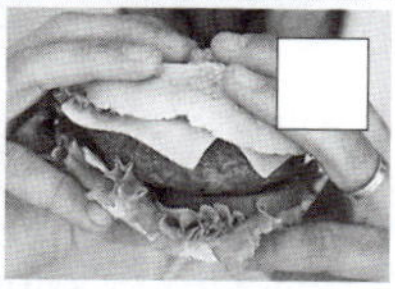

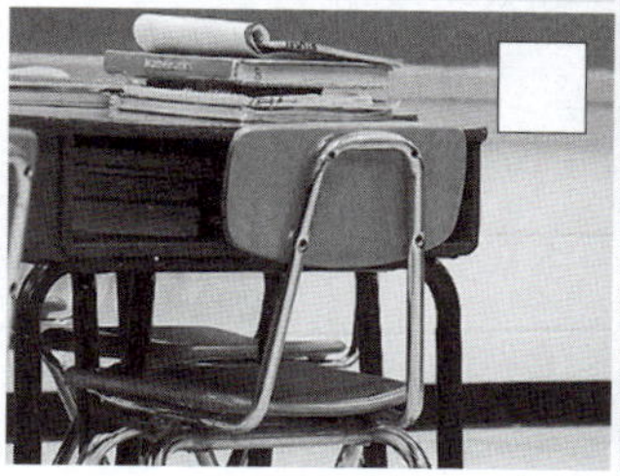

86 Vervollständige die Sätze mit dem jeweils richtigen Wort. Suche dann im Kasten jeweils die Zahl, die zu dem Wort gehört. Verbinde die einzelnen Zahlen miteinander. Die Lösung ergibt ein Bild.

a Would you like ______________ milk in your coffee?
1 some / **2** anything / **3** something

b Rachel doesn't eat ______________ meat.
4 some / **5** any / **6** anything

c Hello, I'm back. Is ______________ at home?
7 something / **8** any / **9** anybody

d They have ______________ chickens in the garden.
10 anything / **11** some / **12** something

e We don't have ______________ to eat this afternoon.
13 something / **14** anything / **15** any

f My sandwich isn't in the fridge. ______________ ate it.
16 somebody / **17** something / **18** any

g Did ______________ watch the film last night?
19 anybody / **20** anything / **21** something

h Tom is reading ______________ pages of his new book.
22 some / **23** something / **24** any

i Is there ______________ cake left?
25 any / **26** anything / **27** something

j Does ______________ know the new song by B & C?
28 something / **29** anybody / **30** any

k She can give me ______________ apples for free.
31 something / **32** somebody / **33** some

l I can see ______________ walking through our garden.
34 some / **35** any / **36** somebody

m We don't know ______________ about our neighbours.
28 something / **9** anything / **5** any

27
24
30
23
2
26
3
21
15
12
22
25
19
10
13
9
33
14
18
16
11
36
29
5
20
4
8
6
35
28
7
17
1
31
32

Wortschatz

87 Tessa hat schon Postkarten aus vielen Ländern bekommen. Aus welchen Ländern stammen die Karten? Wenn du die Buchstaben auf den Bildern in die richtige Reihenfolge bringst, erhältst du den Namen des jeweiligen Landes.

88 An James' Schule gibt es Schüler aus vielen verschiedenen Ländern. Welche Sprache können diese Schüler neben Englisch noch sprechen?

Schreiben

89 Dan und James treffen beim Abendessen zwei Mädchen aus Deutschland. Sie können kaum Englisch. Dan spricht aber gut Deutsch und dolmetscht für James. Was sagt Dan?

MARIE: Ich vermisse das deutsche Essen.

DAN: *She's missing the German food.*

JAMES: Doesn't she like sausages and beans?

DAN: ______________________________

____

MARIE: Ich esse kein Fleisch. Bohnen sind aber in Ordnung.

DAN: ______________________________

____

LISA: Frage James, ob er etwas Obst oder Joghurt möchte.

DAN: ______________________________

____

JAMES: I'd like some fruit.

DAN: ______________________________

____

LISA: O.k., dann hole ich etwas Obst für ihn und natürlich auch für dich.

DAN: Dankeschön!

Topic 11: Training for the competition

There's a big athletic competition in Greenwich in three weeks. Tessa's brother James wants to take part in it. To be fit he eats healthy food and exercises a lot. Here are some tips from his sports teacher Mr Lennon.

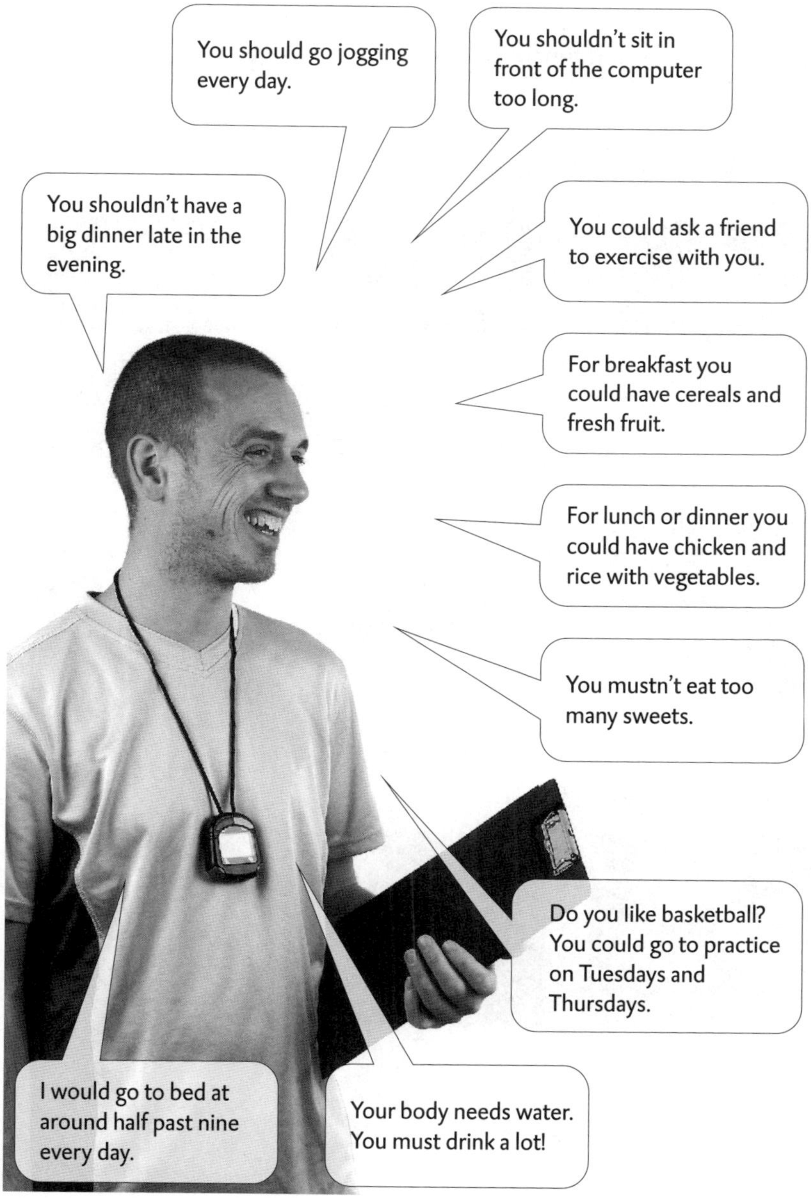

Fragen zum Text

90 Schreibe die richtige Antwort auf oder markiere (✓) das richtige Bild.

a When should James go jogging?

____

b What could he have for lunch?

____

c When is the best time to go to bed?

☐

☐

☐

d James must drink a lot of ______________________.

e What could James eat for breakfast?

☐

☐

☐

f What could James do to keep fit?

☐

☐

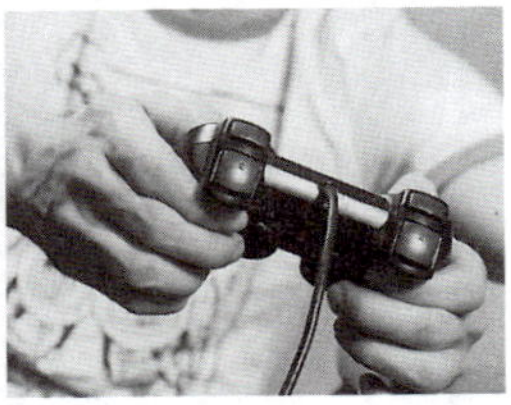
☐

91 James und Tessa unterhalten sich über die Ratschläge des Sportlehrers. James hat dabei einige Tipps falsch verstanden. Schreibe bei den falschen Sätzen jeweils den richtigen Tipp auf, so wie ihn der Trainer gegeben hat.

a "I could go to basketball practice. It's on Tuesdays and Fridays."

____

____

b "Rice and vegetables would be good for dinner."

____

____

c "It's good to eat a lot of food in the evening."

____

____

d "It's better to exercise alone."

____

____

e "Being on the Internet for too long isn't good."

____

____

f "I shouldn't go running daily."

____

____

g "I mustn't eat any sweets."

____

____

Grammatik

Was ist besonders an den Verben *could, would, must* und *should*?

Diese Verben gehören zu den modalen Hilfsverben. Sie haben **immer die gleiche Form** und sie können auch **nicht alleine stehen**, d. h., dass immer auch ein Verb im Infinitiv (Grundform) direkt hinter ihnen stehen muss – außer bei Kurzantworten.

Beispiel: We could watch a film. – Yes, we could.
Wir könnten einen Film ansehen. – Ja, das könnten wir.

Wann verwendest du *could*?

- *Could* ist die **Vergangenheits-Form von *can*** (können).
  Beispiel: When she was young she could play the piano.
  Als sie jung war, konnte sie Klavier spielen.
- *Could* benutzt du auch, wenn du **höflich um etwas bitten** bzw. eine **Möglichkeit** ausdrücken willst.
  Beispiele: Could you close the window, please?
  Könnten Sie / Könntest du bitte das Fenster schließen?
  I could take the bus.
  Ich könnte den Bus nehmen.
- Die **Verneinung** lautet *could not* oder *couldn't*:
  Beispiel: I'm sorry I couldn't come.
  Es tut mir leid, dass ich nicht kommen konnte.

92 Wie sagst du auf Englisch, …

a dass dein Vater sehr schnell laufen konnte, als er jung war.

____

b dass du auch mit dem Zug fahren könntest.

____

c dass ihr schwimmen gehen könntet.

____

d dass James seine Hausaufgaben nicht machen konnte.

____

e dass du die Queen sehen konntest.

____

f Wie bittest du jemanden auf Englisch höflich, ob er/sie nicht die Tür öffnen könnte?

____

____

Wann verwendest du *would*?

- Mit *would* drückt man aus, was man **machen würde oder nicht**.
  Beispiele: I would ride to school by bike.
  Ich würde mit dem Fahrrad zur Schule fahren.
  I would not / wouldn't ride to school by bike.
  Ich würde nicht mit dem Fahrrad zur Schule fahren.
- Auch wenn man jemanden **höflich um etwas bittet oder etwas anbietet**, benutzt man *would*.
  Beispiel: Would you close the window, please?
  Würden Sie / Würdest du bitte das Fenster schließen?
  Would you like a drink?
  Möchten Sie / Möchtest du gerne etwas trinken?

93 James fragt seine Freunde, wie sie sich auf den Wettkampf vorbereiten würden. Hier sind einige Meinungen. Übersetze die fehlenden Satzteile.

a After school ______________________ with a friend.
(... würde ich joggen gehen ...)

b James asked his friend Peter, "______________________

______________________?"
(Möchtest du mit mir joggen gehen?)

c I ______________________ to play basketball with me.
(... würde meine Schwester fragen ...)

d I ______________________ when it's raining.
(... würde nicht trainieren ...)

e James, ______________________ in this competition.
(... ich würde nicht teilnehmen ...)

f We ______________________ in one day.
(... wir würden nicht zu viel Sport machen ...)

Wann verwendest du *must*?

- *Must* wird benutzt, **wenn etwas notwendig** ist oder wenn du ausdrücken willst, **dass etwas getan werden muss**. Du kannst auch eine Form von *have (got) to* verwenden.
  Beispiel: I must tidy up my room. / I have (got) to tidy up my room.
  Ich muss mein Zimmer aufräumen.
- Möchte man eine andere Zeit als das Präsens benutzen, verwendet man statt *must* eine Form von *have to*.
  Beispiel: Last week I had to work at the cinema.
  Letzte Woche musste ich im Kino arbeiten.

Wann verwendest du *mustn't*?

Mustn't wird benutzt, um auszudrücken, dass man etwas **nicht tun darf**.
Beispiel: You mustn't use your dictionary in the test.
Du darfst in der Prüfung dein Wörterbuch nicht benutzen.

94 In der nahe gelegenen Turnhalle mit Sportplatz kann sich James ausgezeichnet auf den Leichtathletik-Wettkampf vorbereiten. Er muss jedoch einige Regeln einhalten. Fasse die Regeln auf Deutsch zusammen.

You mustn't wear outdoor shoes in the sports hall.
You must leave your bag in the changing room.
You mustn't use your phone during training.
Visitors must wait outside the sports hall.
You have to use a towel *(Handtuch)* in training.

95 Trotz des Trainings hilft James im Haushalt mit und darf auch die Schule nicht vernachlässigen. Er berichtet kurz, welche Aufgaben er zu erledigen hat. Setze die modalen Hilfsverben in die richtige Zeit.

Last week I ______________________ (müssen/machen) so much for school. Mr Smith gave us a history text and we __________________ (müssen/lesen) it in just two days. My mum says I __________________ (müssen/lernen) hard because my marks are not very good this year. I ___________________________ (darf nicht/bekommen) a bad mark in the next maths test.

I normally ________________________ (nicht müssen/putzen) the kitchen, but mum was away for the weekend. So Tessa and I cleaned the kitchen. On warm days we both ____________________ (müssen/helfen) in the garden, but I ____________________________ (darf nicht/schneiden) the bushes. Mum says it is too dangerous.

Wann verwendest du *should*?

- *Should* wird verwendet, wenn man einen Rat gibt, jemanden kritisiert oder über Verpflichtungen spricht.
  Beispiele: You should go to bed earlier. — *Du solltest früher ins Bett gehen.*
  You should read more carefully. — *Du solltest genauer lesen.*
- *Should* wird nur in Sätzen im *simple present* verwendet.

96 James' Mutter geht Lebensmittel einkaufen. Aber was soll sie ihrem Sohn mitbringen? Vervollständige ihre Überlegungen.

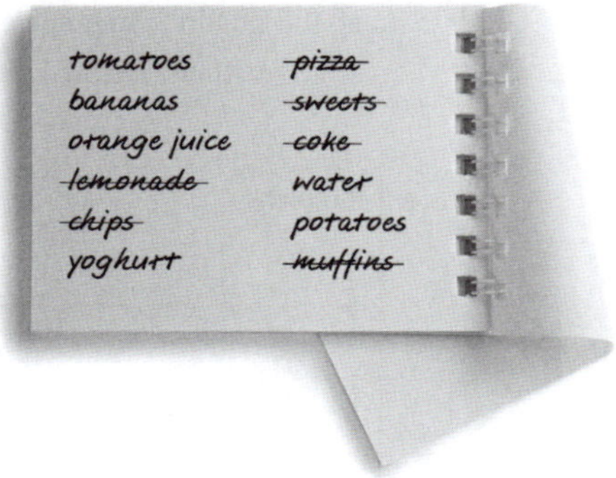

He should eat tomatoes, but he shouldn't eat pizza.

He should ______________________________

____

____

____

____

Wortschatz

97 Im Haushalt gibt es viel zu tun. Sieh dir die Bilder genau an und ordne ihnen die englischen Wörter zu. Kennst du auch die deutsche Bedeutung? Schreibe beides in die Tabelle. Eine Beschreibung passt zu keinem Bild.

to do the laundry | to prepare a meal | to lay the table | to hoover the floor | to wash the dishes | to iron clothes | to take the rubbish out

picture	English	German
a		
b		
c		
d		
e		
f		

98 Setze die gesuchten Begriffe in das Kreuzworträtsel ein. Bringe die umkreisten Buchstaben in die richtige Reihenfolge und notiere das Lösungswort.

Across

1 You have dinner in the … (two words)

3 There could be flowers and bushes in this.

7 Have a rest on the sofa in our … (two words)

8

9 You sleep in this room.

11

13 "Switch on the … It's too dark."

Down

1 To get into the rooms you open the …

4 We keep the bikes in our …

6 You can have a shower here.

8 It should have an oven and a fridge.

10 "It's starting to rain. Quick, shut the …!"

12 "Grandma is calling. Can you answer the …?"

Lösungswort (zwei Wörter):

___ ___ ___ ___ ___   ___ O U ___ ___

Schreiben

99 Welche Aufgaben musst du oder solltest du im Haushalt machen? Schreibe mindestens fünf Sätze mit *must / have (got) to* oder *should*. Versuche auch Wörter aus dem Kasten zu verwenden.

in the morning	every day	at the weekend	in the evening	always	often

Topic 12: The fortune teller

It's the last weekend before the holidays start. Tessa and her friend Robby are at Chelmsford Fair. There are a lot of stalls with food, sweets and funny games. "Look, Tessa. There is a fortune teller this year!" says Robby and points to a big sign:

"That's fun. I'll go in!" Tessa goes into the tent and Robby waits outside.

The fortune teller is an old woman with long, black hair. She is sitting at a round table in front of a shiny crystal ball. "Hello, my dear. Take a seat." Madame Wonder touches the crystal ball and closes her eyes. Tessa begins to feel nervous. "I can see your future: You and a friend will enjoy the fair. For lunch you will have a big snack, but you won't pay for it."
"And what about school?" asks Tessa. Madame Wonder rubs the ball again: "You are a good pupil and you will go to school for only a few more days. Then you can do what you like. That's all I can see. That will be four pounds, please."
Tessa pays and leaves the tent. She walks with Robby to the next food stall and tells him about the fortune teller. At the stall Robby orders two hamburgers with chips. Tessa opens her bag to get out her money.
"Oh, dear. I don't have enough money!"
"That's OK, Tessa. I'll pay for you! Just like the fortune teller said!"
Both start to laugh.

Fragen zum Text

100 Sind die folgenden Sätze wahr *(true)*, falsch *(false)* oder nicht im Text *(not in the text)*? Hake (✓) die richtige Antwort ab.

		true	false	not in the text
a	It's the last weekend before school starts again.	☐	☐	☐
b	At the fair you can also go swimming.	☐	☐	☐
c	Madame Wonder tells the future for £ 4.	☐	☐	☐
d	Tessa goes into the tent with Robby.	☐	☐	☐
e	The fortune teller has got a black cat.	☐	☐	☐
f	Robby will go on holiday with his parents.	☐	☐	☐
g	Tessa orders two hamburgers with chips.	☐	☐	☐
h	Tessa hasn't got enough money for lunch.	☐	☐	☐

101 Bringe die Satzteile in die richtige Reihenfolge. Die Buchstaben am Ende der Sätze ergeben ein Lösungswort.

_____ Robby and Tessa are hungry and want to have lunch. **(u)**

_____ Tessa has to pay £ 4. **(t)**

_____ Tessa doesn't have enough money. **(n)**

__1__ Tessa and Robby are at a fair. **(f)**

_____ Robby pays for Tessa's hamburger. **(e)**

_____ Tessa wants to know about her future. **(o)**

_____ Madame Wonder tells Tessa about her future. **(r)**

Lösungswort: _ _ _ _ _ _ _

Grammatik

Wann verwendest du das *will-future*?

Du verwendest das *will-future*, wenn du:

- **Voraussagen** über zukünftige Ereignisse machen willst.
  Beispiel: It will be a nice party.
- **Vermutungen** äußern willst. Häufig verwendest du dann Ausdrücke wie *probably*, *I think*, *I hope* oder *I'm sure* (Signalwörter).
  Beispiele: I think it will snow tomorrow. *Ich denke, morgen wird es schneien.*
  They will probably go home. *Sie werden wahrscheinlich nach Hause gehen.*
  I'm sure you will pass the test. *Ich bin mir sicher, du wirst den Test bestehen.*
- **spontane Entscheidungen** triffst oder **Versprechen** gibst.
  Beispiele: I'll have a pizza. *Ich nehme eine Pizza.*
  I won't forget you! *Ich werde dich nicht vergessen!*

Wie bildest du das *will-future*?

- Du bildest das *will-future* mit **will + Infinitiv**. *Will* ist für alle Personen gleich.
  Beispiel: I will dance. *Kurzform:* I'll dance. *Ich werde tanzen.*
  He will cook. *Kurzform:* He'll cook. *Er wird kochen.*
- Die **verneinte** Form von *will* lautet **will not**.
  Beispiel: We will not go. *Kurzform:* We won't go. *Wir werden nicht gehen.*

102 Was hat die Wahrsagerin noch in der Glaskugel gesehen? Was wird Tessa heute noch tun oder nicht tun? Schreibe zu den Bildern passende Sätze im *will-future*.

a

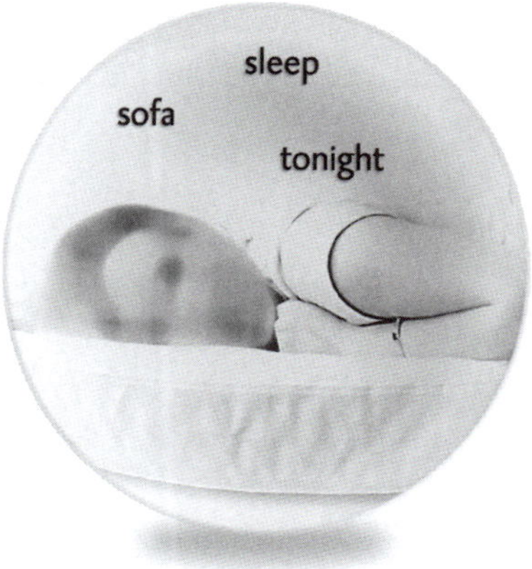

Tessa will sleep on the sofa tonight.

b

She ______________________

____

____

c

Tessa ______________________

____

____

d

She ______________________

____

____

e

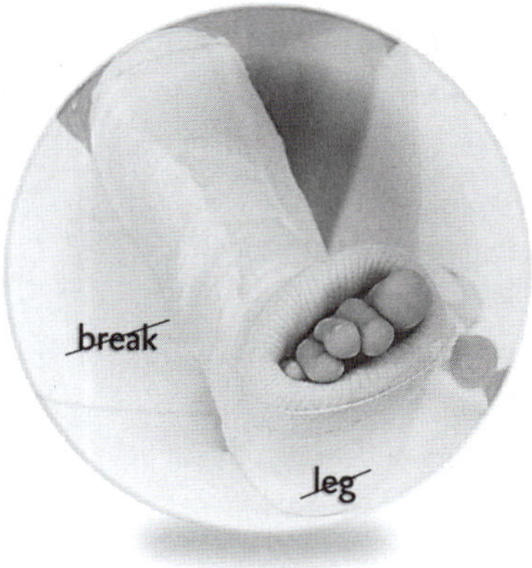

Tessa ______________________________

____

____

f

Tessa ______________________________

____

____

g

She ______________________________

____

____

Wie kannst du Fragen und Kurzantworten im *will-future* bilden?

Die Satzstellung in Fragesätzen ist: ***Will* + Subjekt + Infinitiv + …**

Beispiel: Will you help me?

Möchtest du eine **Kurzantwort** geben, musst du Folgendes beachten:

- Wenn du mit ***yes*** antwortest, musst du die Langform ***will*** verwenden.
  Beispiel: Will you go on holiday? Yes, I will.
- Wenn du mit ***no*** antwortest, verwendest du normalerweise ***won't***.
  Beispiel: Will you eat pizza? No, I won't.

Du kannst auch **Fragewörter** mit dem *will-future* verwenden. Hier musst du nur das Fragewort an den Anfang des Satzes stellen.

Beispiele: Where will Peter go tomorrow?
What will Mary do in the afternoon?

103 Robby und Tessa unterhalten sich über die Wahrsagerin. Robby hat viele Fragen zu Tessas Zukunft. Stelle sie, indem du die Wörter in die richtige Reihenfolge bringst. Formuliere Tessas Antworten.

a you / go / will / to Australia / some day

____?

☺ Yes, *I will*________.

b will / together with / you / Eric / be

____?

☹ No, ____________.

c always / we / be / will / friends

____?

☺ ____________.

d have / will / you / a fast car

____?

☹ ____________.

e you / have / children / will

____?

☺ ____________.

f in Greenwich / we /stay / will / after school

____?

☹ ____________________.

104 Auf dem Heimweg überlegen Tessa und Robby, was sie in den Ferien alles unternehmen können. Bilde mit jedem Fragewort eine Frage zu den möglichen Aktivitäten.

What	will we	go to the swimming pool?
When	won't we	have a picnic?
Why	will I	come with us?
Where	won't I	the film start?
Who	will it	the tickets cost?
	will	your parents say?
	won't you	meet?
		buy a present for Peter's birthday?
		eat a big ice cream?
		go by train?

a ____

b ____

c ____

d ____

e ____

Wortschatz

105 Hier siehst du einige Urlaubsbilder. Welche Wörter gehören zu welchem Bild? Schreibe sie auf die Bilder. Manchmal ist ein Wort auf zwei Bildern zu sehen. Nimm das Wörterbuch erst zu Hilfe, wenn du ein Wort gar nicht kennst.

palm tree   sea   hut   bike trip   camping   tent   camera   book
roller coaster   swimming pool   water slide   hammock   pictures
amusement park   sunglasses   mountains   trees   beach   meadow

Schreiben

106 Stelle dir vor, wie dein Traumurlaub aussehen wird. Verwende das *will-future*. Schreibe,

... wo du hinfahren wirst,
... wo du wohnen wirst,
... mit wem du den Urlaub verbringen wirst,
... was du dort unternehmen wirst.

On my dream holiday I will ...

Vocabulary

Auf den folgenden Seiten kannst du Wörter nachschlagen, die du noch nicht kennst oder die du vergessen hast. Du findest auch eine Übersicht mit unregelmäßigen Verben, die du in der 6. Klasse schon gelernt hast. Am besten prägst du dir den Wortschatz ein, wenn du jeden Tag immer etwa sieben Wörter lernst. Lerne also nicht zu viel auf einmal.
Die Wörter, die neu für dich sind, kannst du in der Vokabelliste und vorne im Text auch markieren. So fallen sie dir gleich auf und du wiederholst sie automatisch.
Du kannst deinen Wortschatz auch erweitern, indem du eine Spalte mit einem Blatt Papier abdeckst und die entsprechenden deutschen oder englischen Wörter oder die unregelmäßigen *simple-past-* und *past-participle*-Formen auf das Blatt schreibst. Sieh dann auch genau nach, ob du die englischen Wörter richtig geschrieben hast.
Die Vokabeln kannst du auch auf Karteikärtchen schreiben. Du kannst dann immer ein paar Vokabeln mitnehmen und sie wiederholen, wenn du Zeit hast.

Vocabulary

Aa	(singing) act	hier: Gesangsnummer
	adult	Erwachsene(r)
	afternoon	Nachmittag
	again	wieder
	almost	beinahe, fast
	a lot of	viel(e)
	always	immer
	a.m./am	*bei Zeitangaben vor 12 Uhr mittags*
	amusement park	Freizeitpark
	animal	Tier
	any	(irgend)ein(e), etwas
	(not) any more	nicht mehr
	anybody	(irgend)jemand
	anything	etwas
	anything else	noch etwas
	apartment (AE)	Wohnung
	apple pie	(gedeckter) Apfelkuchen
	around	rundherum
	(to) arrive	ankommen
	art	Kunst
	athletic	sportlich
	athletics competition	Leichtathletikwettkampf
	autumn (BE)	Herbst
Bb	back	zurück
	balloon	(Luft-)Ballon
	(to) have a barbecue	grillen
	bathroom	Bad, Badezimmer
	Bavarian	bayerisch
	beach	Strand
	bean	Bohne
	beard	Bart
	beautiful	schön
	bedroom	Schlafzimmer
	before	vor
	between	zwischen
	blue	blau

board game	Brettspiel
body	Körper
boot	Stiefel
both	beide
bored	gelangweilt
bottle	Flasche
boyfriend	Freund
break	Pause
breakfast	Frühstück
biscuit (BE)	Keks
bus stop	Bushaltestelle
busy	beschäftigt

Cc

calendar	Kalender
campfire	Lagerfeuer
candy (AE)	Süßigkeiten
candle	Kerze
canoe	Kanu
careful	vorsichtig
caught	gefangen
(to) celebrate	feiern
cereals	Frühstücksflocken
(to) check	kontrollieren, prüfen
checkout	Kasse
cheese	Käse
chicken	Huhn, Hähnchen
children	Kinder
chin	Kinn
chips (BE)	Pommes frites
(to) choose	(aus)wählen
city hall	Rathaus
(to) climb	klettern
(to) close	schließen
clothes	Kleidung
cloudy	bewölkt
coach	Trainer
coast	Küste
coat	Mantel
competition	Wettbewerb

	Congratulations!	Glückwunsch!
	contest	Wettbewerb
	(to) cook	kochen
	cottage	Hütte, Häuschen
	cookie (AE)	Keks, Cookie
	could	konnte, könnte
	(to) count	zählen
	country	Land
	crisps (BE)	Chips
	(to) cross	überqueren
	crystal ball	Kristallkugel
	culture	Kultur
	curly	lockig
	cute	goldig, süß
Dd	dangerous	gefährlich
	date	Verabredung, Datum
	delicious	lecker, köstlich
	diary	Tagebuch
	different	verschieden, unterschiedlich
	dinner	Abendessen
	dining room	Esszimmer
	(to) dive	tauchen
	dot	Punkt
	(to) draw	zeichnen
	(to) drive	Auto fahren
	drums	Schlagzeug
	dry	trocken
	during	während
Ee	early	früh
	(to) eat	essen
	elevator (AE)	Lift, Aufzug
	(to) enjoy	genießen
	enough	genug
	event	Ereignis
	every day	jeden Tag
	exchange programme	Austauschprogramm
	excited	aufgeregt

	(to) exercise	üben, trainieren
	extreme	extrem
	eyebrow	Augenbraue
Ff	fall (AE)	Herbst
	famous	berühmt
	fast	schnell
	favourite	Lieblings-
	feather	Feder
	foot, feet (Pl.)	Fuß, Füße
	festival	Fest
	flat (BE)	Wohnung
	flavour	Geschmack
	floor	Boden, Stockwerk
	flower	Blume
	flute	Flöte
	(to) fly	fliegen
	foggy	neblig
	(to) forget	vergessen
	(to) found	gründen
	fortune teller	Wahrsager(in)
	four times a week	vier mal die Woche
	France	Frankreich
	French	französisch
	Fridays	freitags, am Freitag
	future	Zukunft, zukünftig
Gg	gallery	Galerie
	geography	Geografie, Erdkunde
	German	deutsch, Deutsch (Fach)
	Germany	Deutschland
	glasses	Brille
	(to) glue	kleben
	(to) go across	überqueren
	(to) go along	entlanggehen
	(to) go straight on	geradeaus gehen
	good-looking	gutaussehend
	granddaughter	Enkelin
	great	großartig

	Greece	Griechenland
	Greek	griechisch
	green	grün
	guest list	Gästeliste
	guitar	Gitarre
	gym	Turnhalle
Hh	half past nine	halb zehn
	hammock	Hängematte
	(to) hang out	Zeit verbringen (mit jmd.)
	hat	Hut
	(to) have time	Zeit haben
	healthy	gesund
	(to) hike	wandern
	history	Geschichte
	holidays	Ferien
	(to) hoover	staubsaugen
	hot	heiß
	(to) hurry up	sich beeilen
Ii	indoor	drinnen
	information technology (IT)	Informationstechnologie, Informatik
	in front of	vor
	Irish	irisch
	Irish Pub	irisches Pub
	Irish stew	irischer Eintopf
	(to) iron	bügeln
	Italian	italienisch
	Italy	Italien
Jj	jacket	Jacke
	jam	Marmelade
	jeweller's shop	Juwelier
	(to) join	mitmachen, beitreten
	joke	Witz
	juice	Saft
	jumper	Pullover
	just	gerade, soeben

Kk

karaoke	Karaoke
kitchen	Küche
kite	Flugdrache

Ll

lake	See
Lake District	*Region im Norden Englands*
late	spät
(to) laugh	lachen
laundry	Wäsche
(to) lay	legen
(to) leave	verlassen
library	Bücherei, Bibliothek
lightning	Blitz
living room	Wohnzimmer
lots of	viele
lovely	schön, hübsch, reizend
luckily	glücklicherweise
lunch break	Mittagspause

Mm

maths, mathematics	Mathe, Mathematik
maybe	vielleicht
meadow	Wiese
meal	Mahlzeit
(to) meet	treffen
midnight	Mitternacht
mirror	Spiegel
(to) miss	vermissen, verpassen
modern	modern
Mondays	montags, am Montag
month	Monat
mostly	meist, meistens
motorway	Autobahn
mountain	Berg
must	müssen
mustn't	nicht dürfen

Nn

national park	Nationalpark
neighbour	Nachbar(in)
(to) need	brauchen

	nervous	nervös
	the Netherlands	die Niederlande
	next to	neben
	nope	nein (umgangssprachlich)
	north	Norden, nördlich
Oo	of course	natürlich
	often	oft
	opposite	gegenüber
	(to) order	bestellen
	(to) organise	organisieren, planen
	outside	draußen
	over there	da drüben
Pp	P.E. (Physical Education)	Sport (Fach)
	a pair of trousers	eine Hose
	parade	Parade
	parents	Eltern
	parrot	Papagei
	(to) pay (for)	bezahlen
	(to) perform	aufführen, darbieten
	p.m./pm	*bei Zeitangaben nach 12 Uhr mittags*
	piano	Klavier
	pimple	Pickel
	plate	Teller
	popular	beliebt
	possible	möglich
	potato	Kartoffel
	practice	Training
	(to) practise	üben
	(to) prepare	vorbereiten
	presentation	Präsentation, Referat
	prize	Preis (z. B. in Wettbewerb)
	(to) push	drücken
Rr	rainforest	Regenwald
	(to) remember	sich erinnern
	report	Bericht
	(to) return	zurückgeben

	rice	Reis
	roller coaster	Achterbahn
	roll	Brötchen
	rubbish	Müll
	Russia	Russland
	Russian	russisch
Ss	(to) sail	segeln
	sailing trip	Segeltörn
	sale	Verkauf, Schlussverkauf
	sausage	Wurst
	science	Naturwissenschaften
	sea	Meer
	shark	Hai
	shiny	glänzend
	shoe shop	Schuhgeschäft
	shopping centre	Einkaufszentrum
	should	sollte/solltest/sollten/solltet
	show	Show, Vorstellung
	sight	Sehenswürdigkeit
	sign	Schild, Zeichen
	slime	Schleim
	(to) slobber	sabbern
	smile	Lächeln
	sneakers (AE)	Turnschuhe
	snow	Schnee
	soccer (AE)	(europäischer) Fußball
	soda bread	mit Backpulver gebackenes Brot
	some	einige, ein paar, etwas
	somebody	jemand
	something	etwas
	sometimes	manchmal
	south	Süden, südlich
	Spain	Spanien
	Spanish	spanisch
	(to) spend	(Geld) ausgeben, (Zeit) verbringen
	stall	Stand
	(to) stay	bleiben
	(to) stay up	aufbleiben

	stone	Stein
	strawberry	Erdbeere
	suddenly	plötzlich
	sun cream	Sonnencreme
	sunglasses	Sonnenbrille
	sunny	sonnig
	(to) support	unterstützen
	surprise	überraschen, Überraschung
	sweet	süß
	sweets	Süßigkeiten
	swimming trunks	Badehose
Tt	Take a seat.	Nehmen Sie/Nimm Platz.
	(to) take part	teilnehmen
	(to) take place	stattfinden
	(to) tell	sagen, erzählen
	(to) tell a joke	einen Witz erzählen
	tent	Zelt
	(to) tidy up	aufräumen
	time	Zeit
	tired	müde
	together	zusammen
	tomorrow	morgen
	too long	zu lang
	too many	zu viele
	toothbrush	Zahnbürste
	toothpaste	Zahnpasta
	top	Gipfel, Spitze
	(to) touch	berühren
	toy shop	Spielwarengeschäft
	traffic	Verkehr
	trainers (BE)	Sportschuhe
	(to) travel	reisen
	trumpet	Trompete
	Turkey	Türkei
	(to) turn in	abgeben (z. B. Hausaufgabe)
	(to) turn left/right	nach links/rechts abbiegen

Uu	umbrella	Regenschirm
	unfortunately	unglücklicherweise
	until	bis (zeitlich)
	usually	gewöhnlich
Vv	Valentine's Day	Valentinstag
	vegetables	Gemüse
	view	Ausblick
	(to) visit	besuchen
Ww	water slide	Wasserrutsche
	(to) wear	tragen
	weekend	Wochenende
	whenever	wann immer
	whole	ganz(e/r)
	wife	(Ehe-)Frau
	window	Fenster
	(to) work out	trainieren
	workshop	Arbeitskreis
Yy	you're welcome	bitte, gern geschehen

Auswahl unregelmäßiger Verben

infinitive	simple past	past participle	deutsche Übersetzung
(to) be	was/were	been	*sein*
(to) bring	brought	brought	*bringen*
(to) buy	bought	bought	*kaufen*
(to) come	came	come	*kommen*
(to) cost	cost	cost	*kosten*
(to) do	did	done	*tun, machen*
(to) drink	drank	drunk	*trinken*
(to) eat	ate	eaten	*essen*
(to) fall	fell	fallen	*fallen*
(to) find	found	found	*finden*
(to) get	got	got	*bekommen, werden*
(to) go	went	gone	*gehen*
(to) have	had	had	*haben*
(to) have to	had to	had to	*müssen*
(to) make	made	made	*machen*
(to) meet	met	met	*treffen*
(to) put	put	put	*setzen, stellen, legen*
(to) read	read	read	*lesen*
(to) run	ran	run	*laufen*
(to) say	said	said	*sagen*
(to) see	saw	seen	*sehen*
(to) sell	sold	sold	*verkaufen*
(to) sit	sat	sat	*sitzen*
(to) sleep	slept	slept	*schlafen*
(to) speak	spoke	spoken	*sprechen*
(to) swim	swam	swum	*schwimmen*
(to) take	took	taken	*nehmen*
(to) think	thought	thought	*denken, glauben*
(to) understand	understood	understood	*verstehen*
(to) win	won	won	*gewinnen*
(to) write	wrote	written	*schreiben*

Key

Dieses Kapitel enthält die Lösungen zu allen Aufgaben. Damit du sie schneller findest, wurden viele der Lösungen **fett hervorgehoben**. Manchmal gibt es mehr als nur eine einzige richtige Lösung. Die verschiedenen Lösungsmöglichkeiten sind dann durch Schrägstriche voneinander getrennt. Die Lösungen zur Textproduktion sind als Vorschlag zu verstehen. Lass dich daher nicht entmutigen, wenn deine Lösung von der im Buch angegebenen abweicht! Prüfe auch deine Rechtschreibung genau. Wenn deine Lösung falsch war, solltest du die Aufgabe später noch einmal wiederholen.

Topic 1: My dream life

1

2

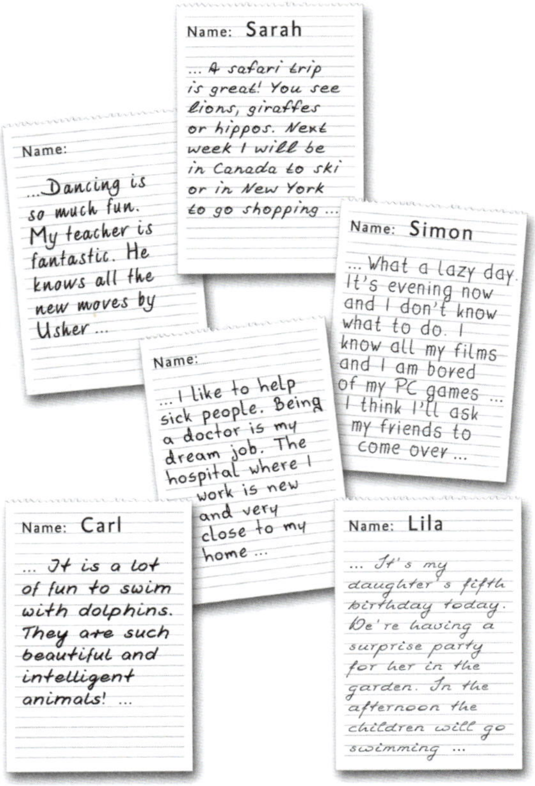

3 **a** Simon: “I eat chocolate and crisps for lunch.”
Simon eats chocolate and crisps for lunch.

b Tom: “I play football for Manchester United.”
Tom plays football for Manchester United.”

c Carl: “In the evenings I go climbing.”
Carl goes climbing in the evenings.

d Lila: “I swim with my children in the sea.”
Lila swims with her children in the sea.

e Sarah: “In the cities I see many famous sights.”
Sarah sees many famous sights in the cities.

f Jenny: “I am a doctor and help people.”
Jenny is a doctor and helps people.

g Arthur: “To keep fit I do some sport before breakfast.”
To keep fit Arthur does some sport before breakfast.

4 *Beispiele:*
On Monday Sarah listens to music.
On Tuesday Simon and Lisa hang out with friends.
On Wednesday Carl surfs the Internet.
On Thursday Lila and Lucy draw pictures.
On Friday Tom and Jerry go to the cinema.
On Saturday Jenny reads magazines.
On Sunday Arthur and Barry take the dog for a walk.

5 **a** Dominic **doesn't** watch sad movies. He **watches** funny movies.
b Livia **doesn't live** in Berlin. She **lives** in Cologne.
c We **don't eat** meat. We only **eat** vegetables.
d Your clothes **don't smell** nice. They **smell** bad.
e John **doesn't go** to school by train. He and a friend **go** by bus.
f I **don't meet** my girlfriend in the city. I **meet** her at home.
g Anthony's mum **doesn't tidy up** his room. Anthony **tidies up** his room himself.

6 **a** **Does** Jenny cook dinner on Wednesday? – **Yes,** she **does**.
b **Does** Tom play the guitar? – **Yes**, he **does**.
c **Does** Jenny go ice-skating on Monday? – **No**, she **doesn't**.
d **Do** Steve and Rob watch DVDs? – **Yes**, they **do**.

e **Does** Jenny play hockey? – **No, she doesn't.**
f **Do** Bea and Steve learn French ? – **Yes, they do.**
g **Do** Tom and Jenny play volleyball together? – **No, they don't.**
h **Does** Tom clean his mum's car on Thursday? – **No, he doesn't.**

7 a FRIENDS: **Do** the earthlings also **play** spaceball?
MIKA: No, **they don't**. They **play football.**

b FRIENDS: **Do** the earthlings also **swim** in slime?
MIKA: No, **they don't**. **They swim** in water.

c FRIENDS: **Does** a child from planet Earth also like to **eat** worms?
MIKA: A child from planet Earth **doesn't eat** worms! The children like to **eat ice-cream**, for example.

d MIKA: The earthlings **don't watch** space ships. They **watch TV**.

e MIKA: The earthlings like to **listen to** music.
FRIENDS: What is music? We **don't** know what that is.

8
- play chess
- collect stamps
- play the guitar
- fly a kite
- take pictures
- play computer games
- go shopping
- play table tennis
- go ice-skating

9 My **dog** does my **homework**

My **dog** does my **homework** at home every **night**. He answers each **question and** gets them all **right**.
There's only **one** problem with **homework** by Rover. I can't turn in **work** that's been slobbered all over.

Topic 2: Back to school

10 **a** Where do the pupils eat their lunch?

 ☐

 ☑

 ☐

b What is Tessa's favourite dessert?

 ☐

 ☐

 ☑

c Mr Miller is the coach of which team?

 ☑

 ☐

 ☐

d What is Paula doing?

 ☐

 ☑

 ☐

11 a Pupils can have a snack every (**lunch**) **break**.
b Peter and Sam often **play basketball**.
c Tessa usually does sports on **Mondays** and **Fridays**.
d The school club doesn't meet in the afternoon.
They meet **in the evening**.
e Kim **is reading** a book in the library.
f In the **music room** you can sing karaoke.
g Mrs Dough works **in the** (**school**) **kiosk**.
h The kiosk isn't **open** at the weekend.

12 Today most pupils are eating pizza.
They are also selling ice-cream (this afternoon).
Peter and Sam are playing basketball now.
At the moment Kim is reading a book.
Paula is singing karaoke (in the music room).

13 a A pupil **is** reading a book.
b The pupils **are** listening to the teacher.
c John is **writing/reading** a text message on his mobile phone.
d A man and a woman **are looking** out of the train window.
e The boy **is sleeping** during the lesson.
f Zoe and Steve **are watching TV.**

14 a Tim is writing a story.
He **is not/isn't writing** an e-mail.

b Vera and Meg are cleaning their bikes
They **are not/aren't cleaning** their mopeds.

c Kim is opening the door.
She **is not/isn't opening** the window.

d Dad and I **are not/aren't working** in the garden.
We are working in the garage.

e I **am not/I'm not learning** Spanish.
I am learning French and English.

f You are drawing a farm.
You **are not/aren't drawing** a city.

g Tina is arriving home at 7 pm.
She **is not/isn't arriving** home at 7 am.

15 a **Are** you **riding a horse**?
– **Yes, I am**.

b **Are** we **going to the cinema** now?
– Yes, **we are**.

c **Are** you **buying a skirt**?
– No, **I'm not**. / **I am not**.

d **Is** Felix **playing with a friend**?
– Yes, **he is**.

e **Are** Emma and Terry **enjoying the trip?**
– No, **they aren't**.

16 SUE: Hi Aunt Sally. How are you? I**'m calling** to tell you about my first day back at school.

AUNT: Hello, my dear. Thanks for calling. Any news?

SUE: There's a new girl called Tessa in my class. She's very nice and plays basketball. Our school team **is looking** for new players. Maybe she can join the club. Anyway, what are **you doing** right now?

AUNT: **I'm cleaning** the bathroom and your uncle **is working** outside. There is always something to do in the garden.

SUE: I know. Dad **is cutting** the bushes at the moment. And Mum **is going** to town now.

AUNT: Why **is** she **going** to town?

SUE: She needs a nice dress for tomorrow night. There's a festival.

AUNT: Oh, nice. And you **aren't helping** your dad?

SUE: No, **I'm not**, I don't have time. Chloe, a friend from school, **is waiting** for me. We**'re writing** a report about a new computer game.

AUNT: OK, my love. Thanks for your call.

SUE: You're welcome. Bye bye.

17

TIMETABLE

NAME: *Tessa Owen* YEAR: 8

Monday	Tuesday	Wednesday	Thursday	Friday
English	English	Geography	Physical Education (P.E.)	Maths
Maths	German	Maths	Physical Education (P.E.)	Science
Science	History	English	Maths	History
LUNCH BREAK				
German	Music	Art	Information Technology (IT)	English

18

alcrmooss

classroom

mgy

gym

titleos

toilets

rmoocmopetur

computer room

icftearea

cafeteria

cmiusomor

music room

yblirar

library

iktnehc

kitchen

dnegar

garden

19 Hi Linda,

I want to tell you about my first **day** at my new school. Mrs Glinn is my favourite **teacher**. She teaches **Art** in our class one day a week. You know it's my favourite **subject**. I love painting and drawing pictures!
The school is really good. There's a big **library** where you can sit and read books. Right now **I'm/am writing** this mail to you in the **computer room**. It is very modern and you can surf the Internet whenever you like. During break you can **play** football or other games outside. Next week I'm going to the **basketball** club. I'm so excited!
And I've got a new friend. Her **name** is Sue. She is really nice.

Take care!

Love, Tessa

Topic 3: Who was it?

20

Emily

Mrs Clark and Emma

Mr Evans and Sarah

Mr Steel

Mr and Mrs Adams

George

21

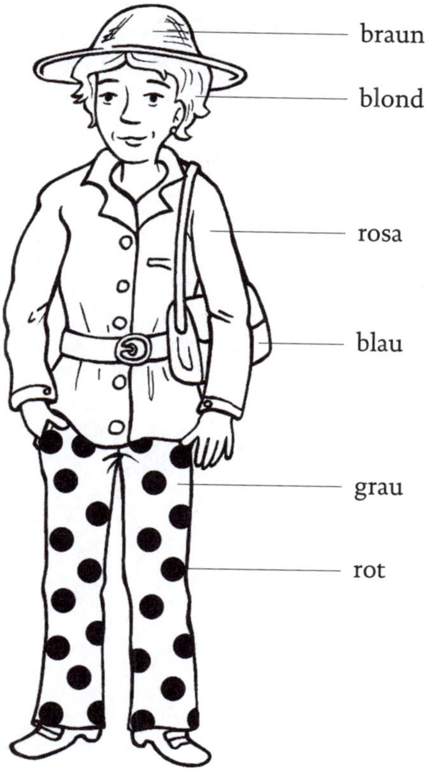

22

- [ ] Sarah bought a teddy bear.
- [x] Mrs Smith has got three children.
- [x] Mrs Clark is Emma's grandma.
- [ ] Emily's boyfriend has got three dogs.
- [x] Mrs Steel was in the shoe shop.
- [ ] Mr Evans ate fast food in the shopping centre.
- [x] The woman ran into Simon.
- [ ] Mr Steel drank tea in a café.

23

a Tom's favourite music is hip hop. **He** listens to music all day.
b Greg and Joshua play the guitar. **They** meet three times a week.
c Evie is a music fan, but **she** can't play an instrument.

d Everyone listens to Radio FM 105. **It** plays a lot of popular songs.
e A friend and I are going to a concert. **We** got the tickets for Christmas.
f The two girls are good at playing the piano. **They** practise a lot.
g Hannah asks Tom: "Do **you** want to dance?"
h Lisa's friend Simon likes sports. **He** always watches football on TV.

24 a How old are Ethan and Evie?
They're twelve years old.

b Is blue your favourite colour?
Yes, it is.

c Where is Millie today?
She is at her aunt's house.

d Ben and Jerry, are you ready for dinner?
Yes, we're so hungry!

e Would you like to visit me?
I would love to.

25 a Clara explains the exercise to <u>her friend Louise</u>.
☐ us ☐ me ☑ her

b They don't know <u>the film</u>.
☑ it ☐ you ☐ them

c Ann is writing an e-mail to <u>Fred</u>.
☐ her ☐ me ☑ him

d Yesterday Theo called <u>Jane</u>.
☐ him ☐ it ☑ her

e Grandma bought some sweets for <u>her grandchildren</u>.
☐ us ☐ you ☑ them

f Close <u>the door</u>, please.
☐ her ☑ it ☐ them

g Can you show <u>my brother and me</u> how it works?
☐ you ☑ us ☐ them

26 **a** Where is Liam? Have you seen **him**?
b Phoebe and Oscar have got some new games. They often play **them**.
c "Daisy, can I come with **you**. I've missed the bus."
d We're at home tonight. Sue can call **us**.
e Megan is a good friend of mine. I like **her** a lot.
f I'm going to town. Do you want to come with **me**?
g Teacher: "Max and Jake, I can hear **you** talking!"
h "Believe **me**, I know where to go."

27

butcher

shoe shop

car park

market

restaurant

28 LADY: Excuse me, maybe you can help me. How do I get to the bus stop where the buses to the city centre stop?

YOU: Well, you **cross Market Road. Then you cross Broad Street. Go along Broad Street until you see the bus stop on your left.**

LADY: Oh, thank you. I'm going to see my granddaughter and I would like to bring her a book. Is there also a book shop nearby?

YOU: Yes, there is. We're at the station now, and you **turn left into Garden Road and then turn left again into Steel Street. The book shop is next to the butcher's**.

LADY: Can I get a coffee there?

YOU: No, I don't think so. But there is a café in Broad Street. **Turn left into Broad Street und go straight on** until you see the café on your left.

LADY: Great! Could you tell me how to get to the bus stop from the café?

YOU: That's easy. It's just **opposite** the café.

LADY: Thank you very much.

29 *Lösungsbeispiele:*

hair	body	clothes	face
• *long*	• athletic	• *trousers*	• *small nose*
• *short*	• *thin*	• *skirt*	• *big eyes*
• *blonde*	• *big*	• *jacket*	• *pimples*
• *brown*	• *short*	• *coat*	• *thin eyebrows*
• *curly*	• *tall*	• *jumper*	• *glasses*

30 *Lösungsbeispiele:*

The police are looking for …

a small lady with short, brown hair. Her eyebrows are thin, her eyes are brown and she wears glasses. She is about 50 to 60 years old. She is wearing a coat and a dress with flowers on it. The lady has got a blue umbrella with her.

a boy with long black hair. He's got green eyes and a thin beard on his chin. The boy is about 18 years old. He is wearing a T-shirt and blue jeans with pockets on them. He is also wearing a necklace and a blue cap.

Topic 4: A trip to the Lake District

31 a On Friday afternoon Tessa, Sue and Sue's parents **started their tour.**
b After dinner they played games and **talked for a long time.**
c It was a sunny Saturday morning so **they hiked to the top of a mountain.**
d After lunch they **did a canoe tour.**
e When Tessa tried to stand up in the canoe **she almost fell into the water.**
f At the market **Tessa bought some cheese.**
g Tessa and Sue slept on the way home because **they were so tired.**

32 a

We played some board games.

b

We hiked to the top of a mountain.

c

We saw wild animals.

d

We put our feet in the water.

e

We made a campfire. /
We grilled sausages.

f

We went on a bike trip.

33

deutsche Grundform	englische Grundform	past tense
arbeiten	work	worked
reden	talk	talked
öffnen	open	opened
helfen	help	helped
zu Fuß gehen	walk	walked
spielen	play	played
springen	jump	jumped
ansehen	watch	watched
anrufen	call	called

34

On Friday afternoon Dad worked in the garden and James helped him to cut the bushes. Later I walked to the shops to buy food for dinner. In the evening Dad and I watched the new film with Will Smith. It was really good. On Saturday morning I heard a strange noise. I opened the window and our neighbour's little black cat jumped into the house. That was a surprise! James played with it until lunch. In the early evening I called your grandma. We talked for a long time. She's fine and wants you to visit her soon. Well, let's have dinner now.

35 unregelmäßige Verben: **was/be, went/go, had/have, took/take, saw/see, did/do**

regelmäßige Verben: **walked/tried/packed**

36 Last Saturday *was* (be) great. My best friend Tom *had* (have) a birthday party in his garage. His parents *gave* (give) him a big TV as a present. From his friends he *got* (get) some new DVDs. I *bought* (buy) him a computer game. All the guests *were* (be) really nice. We *ate* (eat) a lot of pizza and cake and *drank* (drink) cola and lemonade. At midnight I *went* (go) home by bike.

37 Tessa had a lovely weekend. She brought home some souvenirs from the Lake District: For her mum she picked a bunch of **flowers** from the meadow behind the cottage. At the market she bought some **cheese** for her dad, who loves to eat it with salty crackers and grapes. He also got a jar of strawberry **jam**. Next to this present there are four **apples**. Tessa got them from a farmer. The **stones** in front of the suitcase are for James. They are from the lake Tessa and her friend swam in.
The weather was great and so Tessa needed her **hat** and a pair of **sunglasses**. Just before they started back home Tessa had found a beautiful duck's **feather**. She wants to glue it into her diary.

38 *Lösungsbeispiele:*

a On Friday evening I called a friend.
b We watched a new show on TV.
c On Saturday it was my birthday. I had a big party.
d On Sunday I played football, but my team lost.
e In the evening I did my maths homework.

Topic 5: The exchange student

39

☑

☑

☑

☐

☐

40 St. Patrick is always on **17th March**. It is said that Patrick died on that day in 461. People celebrate the fact that he brought his religion to Ireland and founded **schools** and **churches**. Irish people all over the world have **parades** on that day. The oldest parade is in **New York**. Lots of **bands** play music and you can eat **delicious/typical** Irish food.

41
- **a** I **didn't ride** my bike to school today.
- **b** We **didn't get** tickets for the concert.
- **c** Dan **didn't go** out with his friends last night.
- **d** Matt **didn't do** his history project.
- **e** Lisa **didn't eat** much cake at the party.
- **f** Theo **didn't play** football with his friends because he was ill.

42
- **a** We weren't in the city yesterday.
- **b** The weather wasn't great.
- **c** There wasn't a farmer's market on Saturday.
- **d** My friends weren't too lazy to go shopping.

43
- **a** Yes, we did.
- **b** No, you didn't.
- **c** Yes, he did.
- **d** No, I didn't.
- **e** Yes, she did.
- **f** Yes, they did.
- **g** No, it didn't.

44
- **a** **Did** you meet Tessa's friends? Yes, **I did**.
- **b** **Did** Tessa go to school with you on the first day? **Yes, she did.**
- **c** **Did** her parents show you around town? **Yes, they did.**
- **d** **Did** you buy all your school books last week? **No, I didn't.**
- **e** **Did** you go to the tennis club? **No, I didn't.**
- **f** **Did** you miss us? **Yes, I did.**

45
- **a** **Where did** you go to school?
- **b** **Who did** you meet in town?
- **c** **What did** you eat for breakfast?
- **d** **How did** you like the game?
- **e** **When did** you leave the house?
- **f** **Why didn't** she call me?

46

biscuits		*cookies*
crisps		*chips*

football		soccer
sweets		candy
flat		apartment
autumn		fall
lift		elevator
trainers		sneakers

47

a	They are made of potatoes.	**chips**
b	It's a popular sport in Germany.	**soccer**
c	They are in all tall buildings.	**elevators**
d	Halloween and Thanksgiving are in this season.	**fall**
e	It's a place to live in.	**apartment**

48 JOHN: Did you like it in England?
SEAN Yes, I liked it a lot/very much.
LISA: Did you meet Tessa's friends?
SEAN: Yes, I met them. They are very nice.
JOHN: Did you go to a party?
SEAN: No, we didn't. But we went to a pop concert.
DAVID: Did you do any sports?
SEAN: Yes, I played hockey.
LISA: When did school start?
SEAN: It always started at 9 a.m.
JOHN: Did you miss America?
SEAN: I often thought about home.

Topic 6: A date on Valentine's Day

49

		true	false	not in the text
a	Jonathan is the funniest boy at school.	☐	☑	☐
b	Jonathan is younger than Eric.	☐	☑	☐
c	Tessa is Jonathan's neighbour.	☑	☐	☐
d	Jonathan has got two younger brothers.	☐	☑	☐
e	Eric and Jonathan are friends.	☐	☐	☑
f	Jonathan is good at sports.	☑	☐	☐
g	Eric's hair is shorter than Jonathan's hair.	☐	☑	☐
h	Eric is shorter than Jonathan.	☑	☐	☐
i	Tessa and Eric like the same food.	☐	☐	☑
j	Eric likes music better than sports.	☑	☐	☐

50

51

cheap	*cheaper*	*(the) cheapest*
hard	*harder*	(the) hardest
hot	*hotter*	*(the) hottest*
old	*older*	(the) oldest
nice	*nicer*	*(the) nicest*
dry	drier	*(the) driest*
busy	*busier*	(the) busiest

52

expensive	*more expensive*	*(the) most expensive*
important	*more important*	*(the) most important*
interesting	*more interesting*	(the) most interesting

53
a Bob is strong but Timothy is **stronger**. Clive is the **strongest**.
b My new trainers were cheap but Alan's new shoes were **cheaper**. Ann's sandals were **the cheapest**.

- **c** Did Joey get many presents for Christmas? Yes, he did. But Samuel got **more** and Lilly got **(the) most**.
- **d** Susie's cocoa is hot. Dan's cocoa is **hotter**. Olivia's tea is **the hottest**.
- **e** Lisa's hair is short but Peter's hair is **shorter**. Peter's brother has got **the shortest** hair.
- **f** Our house is old but Grandma's house is **older**. My aunt's house is **the oldest**.
- **g** Simon's shirts are dirty. The white shirt is the **dirtiest**.
- **h** Ruth has got three younger brothers. Finn is **the youngest**.
- **i** Rome and Paris are big cities in Europe, but London is **bigger** and Moscow is **the biggest** city in Europe.
- **j** I'm good at Biology, but I'm **better** at Geography. I'm **best** at Maths.
- **k** Mr Tuck's rubbish smells really bad. Mrs Taylor thinks her bin smells **worse** and Mr Todd's rubbish smells **(the) worst**.

54
- **a** I think volleyball is boring. Football is **more exciting**.
- **b** The **most boring** sport is golf.
- **c** The Beatles are the **most famous** pop band.
- **d** I think sharks are the **most dangerous** animals in the sea.
- **e** The flat isn't cheap, but the house is **more expensive**.

55
- **a** A ticket for Movie Night is **cheaper than** a ticket for the Super Bowling.
- **b** Movie Night ends **later than** the Super Bowling.
- **c** The School Concert takes **longer than** the Super Bowling.
- **d** For the Super Bowling you have to be **older than** for the School Concert.
- **e** Movie Night starts **earlier than** the Super Bowling.

56
a

small	–	**tall**	left	–	**right**
mother	–	**father**	daughter	–	**son**
black	–	**white**	warm	–	**cold**
bitter	–	**sweet**	upstairs	–	**downstairs**
slowly	–	**fast**	dirty	–	**clean**
come	–	**go**	poor	–	**rich**
day	–	**night**	hello	–	**goodbye**

b People can be tall or **small**.
They all live on a big, round ball.

Some people are very old,
the weather can be warm or **cold**.

There was a big fight
in the street last **night**.

I have to **go**
and leave the show.

The moon and stars are in the sky,
don't forget to say **goodbye**.

57 Hi Ben,

I hope you're fine. I went out with a girl **last night. Her name is Tessa and she is 12 years old. She has got blue eyes and long, dark hair. We went to Movie Night at school on Valentine's Day. We had so much fun. Tessa is great!**

Write soon,
Eric

Topic 7: A birthday surprise

58 Shopping list: **coke, lemonade, sausages, rolls, sweets, crisps, chocolate ice-cream, candles, balloons**

59 a

b

c

d

e

f

60
- **a** Tessa's family buys a lot of/lots of things for the party.
- **b** Tessa gets a lot of/lots of presents on her birthday. / On her birthday Tessa gets a lot of/lots of presents.
- **c** There are a lot of/lots of people in the supermarket.
- **d** You can buy a lot of/lots of sweets in the shop.
- **e** A lot of/Lots of Tessa's friends will come to the party.

61

much	many
coke	people
time	sausages
ice-cream	rolls
money	sweets

62

a
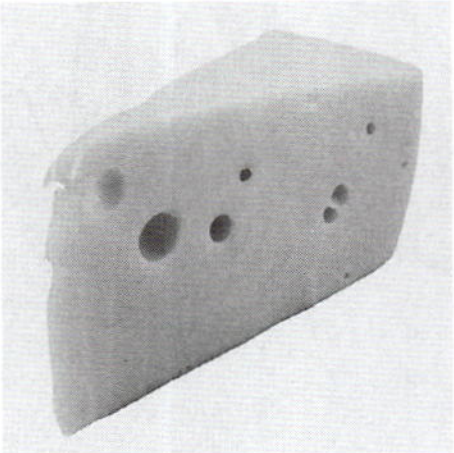
much cheese

b

much rain

c

many flowers

d

many eggs

e

many cards

f

many pencils

g

many bananas

h

much butter

i

much money

63

a There are **a lot/lots of** guests in the room.
b Tessa's parents didn't buy too **much** lemonade.
c How **many** candles are on the cake?
d I got so **many** presents! Thank you!
e How **many** CDs have we got?
f Did Tessa's mother make **many** cakes for the party?

g There are **a lot of/lots of** boys and girls from Tessa's class at the party.
h How **much** money did you get?
i **A lot of/Lots of** guests have to go home early.
j There isn't **much** coke left at the end of the party.

64
1 orange juice
2 lemonade/mineral water
3 cake
4 glass
5 spoon
6 fork
7 rolls
8 sausages
9 plates
10 knife
11 crisps
12 ice-cream

Folgende Dinge kannst du zum Beispiel noch hinzufügen:
candles, balloons, chocolate, jelly babies

65 strawberry apple potatoes tea jam pasta
salad fruit beans chicken fish milk

a I love to eat **strawberry** ice-cream.
b Susy eats her cornflakes with lots of **milk**.
c An **apple** a day keeps the doctor away.
d My mother puts sugar and milk in her **tea**.
e For breakfast Julian wants to have bread and butter and **jam**.
f The Italians are famous for their delicious **pasta**.
g Chips are made from **potatoes**.

66 Dear Pete,

It's my 13th birthday next week. The party is in the bowling centre on Friday, 19th January. We meet at 7 pm. I hope you've got time to come.
Please answer as soon as possible!

Yours, Mike

Topic 8: What's next?

67
a It's the school concert.
b Steve's birthday is first.
c It's Zoe's birthday.
d They have (got) eight days.

e He's three days older.

f They are holidays.

68

JUNE						
1 Internet workshop	**2** start writing book report	**3**	**4**	**5** Steve (12)	**6**	**7**
8 Eric (12)	**9** Maths exam 1st lesson	**10** book report presentation	**11**	**12** school concert	**13**	**14**
15 trip to the National Museum	**16**	**17**	**18** no school!	**19** History test	**20**	**21**
22 Zoe (13)	**23**	**24**	**25** sports day	**26**	**27**	**28**
29 holiday!	**30** holiday!					

69 *The Blue Eyes* are in **first** place.
They won every match!
The **second** best team is *Nightmare.*
The Lucky Six are in **third** place.
Goals 4U are in **fourth** place,
The Elephants came **fifth**,
The Chatterboxes came **sixth**
and *The Socks* are in **seventh** place.
They didn't win any match.
Congratulations to the winning team!

70

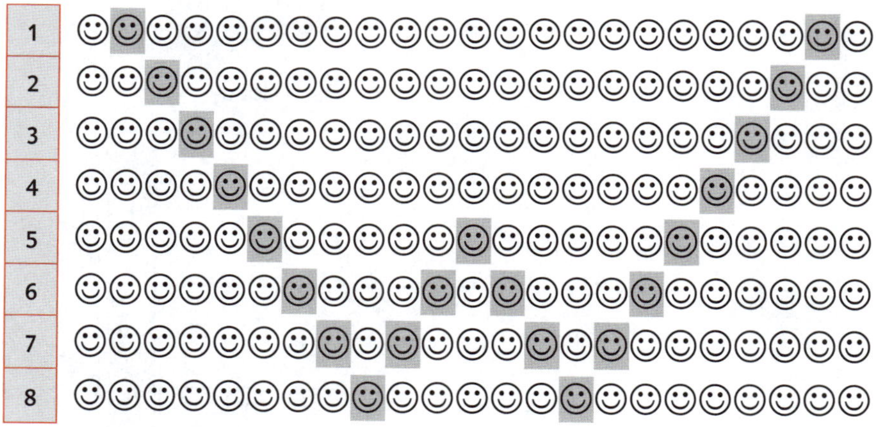

examples:

a water
b win
c weather
d world
e what

71

9th April	**23rd Jan**	**11th April**	**18th Dec**	**1st May**	**21st Jan**	**5th Jan**
S		U		R	P	
18th Mar	**21st Aug**	**13th Dec**	**2nd Jan**	**9th Mar**	**19th Aug**	
R		I	S		E	

birthday **surprise**

72
- **a** November, December, **January**, February
- **b** nineteenth, twentieth, **twenty-first**, twenty-second
- **c** Sunday, Monday, Tuesday, **Wednesday**
- **d** second, third, fourth, **fifth**
- **e** Wednesday, Thursday, **Friday**, Saturday
- **f** March, April, **May**, June

73

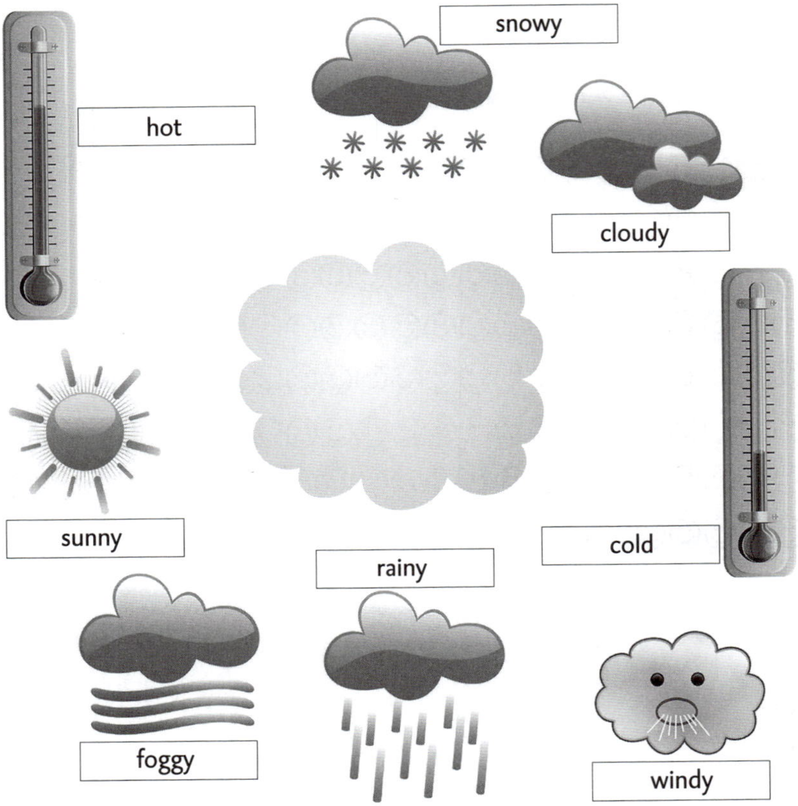

74 Hi Nick,

Yesterday was the talent show at my school. It was so much fun. The top four were great. In first place was **Lisa**. She **sang, "My heart will go on"**. It was fantastic! In **second place was the clever dog Itsy**. **He did funny tricks. Kevin was in third place. He danced like Justin Timberlake! He's a good dancer. Tim and Peter were in fourth place. They've got an interesting talent. They can make music with glasses. Maybe I can learn how to do it.** And how was your week?

Topic 9: The website

75
- **a** Contact us
- **b** About us
- **c** Library
- **d** Gallery
- **e** Teachers
- **f** Downloads

76 **The talent show**

In the last week of April our school ~~organisd~~ a talent show. **organised**
20 pupils aged ~~betwen~~ 12 and 16 showed the jury ~~there~~ best talent. **between, their**
Lots of people didn't want to miss this event and supported ~~they're~~ favourite acts. **their**
Most of them were ~~famous~~ acts, of course. **singing**
Boys and girls sang famous songs from the charts,
but there were also great hip hop dances.
The winner of our show ~~weren't~~ a pupil. **wasn't**
Max, a boy from Year 8, ~~took~~ his parrot "Cheeky", ~~which~~ could count, sing, dance and do acrobatic tricks. **brought**, **who** (der Papagei hat einen Namen, deshalb: *who*)
The jury decided that he was the winner of the show. Congratulations!

77

English	German
last week of April	letzte Aprilwoche (Woche im April)
lots of pupils	viele Schüler
most of them	die meisten (davon)
the winner of our talent show	der Gewinner des Talentwettbewerbs
pictures of the talent show	Bilder des Talentwettbewerbs

78
- **a** The last letter of the alphabet is "z".
- **b** The first day of the week is Monday. / Monday is the first day of the week.
- **c** Munich is the name of a Bavarian city. /
  The name of a Bavarian city is Munich.

d Peter is the winner of the game. / The winner of the game is Peter.
e The colour of the sofa is green. / Green is the colour of the sofa.
f The title of the song is “Back Home”. / “Back Home” is the title of the song.

79
a My parents often drink a **cup of** tea for breakfast.
b Fred is thirsty. He needs a big **glass of/bottle of** water.
c Mum cut up apples, strawberries and melons this morning. Now there is a **bowl of** fruit in the fridge.
d I don’t like black coffee. I put a **lot of/a spoon** of sugar in the cup.
e Angela went shopping. She went home with a **bag of** clothes.
f Chris isn’t hungry any more. He ate a **plate of** steak and fries.
g Can I have a **bottle of/glass of** coke, please?
h There are **a lot of** children in our neighbourhood.

80

t**r**u**mp**et	d**r**u**m**s
v**i**o**l**in	g**u**it**a**r
ce**ll**o	f**l**ut**e**
sa**x**op**h**o**n**e	p**i**a**n**o

81 *Beispiele:*
a I like hip hop.
b My favourite singer is Justin Bieber.
c I like Maroon 5 best.
d My favourite song is “Easy”.
e I listen to music on the bus and at home.
f My mum likes jazz and my dad listens to classical music.

Topic 10: Packing a bag

82

☑

☐

☑

[x]

[ ]

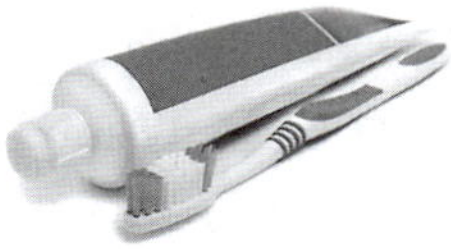

[x]

[ ]

[x]

[ ]

83
- **a** (two pairs of) shorts
- **b** a jacket
- **c** (two pairs of) swimming trunks
- **d** shampoo
- **e** (two) pullovers
- **f** glasses

84
- **a** Mike meets **some** friends in front of the cinema.
  Mike trifft sich mit ein paar Freunden vor dem Kino.
- **b** Would you like **some** chocolate?
  Möchtest du gerne etwas Schokolade?
- **c** Could you give me **some** salt for my egg, please?
  Könntest du mir bitte etwas Salz für mein Ei geben?
- **d** There isn't **any** water in the fridge.
  Es ist kein Wasser im Kühlschrank.
- **e** I don't have **any** salami, but I can give you **some** cheese.
  Ich habe keine Salami, aber ich kann dir (**etwas**) **Käse geben.**

85 (A) "Can somebody help me, please?"
(B) "Is it anybody's birthday?"
(C) "Look, there is something on the table."
(D) "There isn't anything on the table."
(E) "Can I have something to drink?"

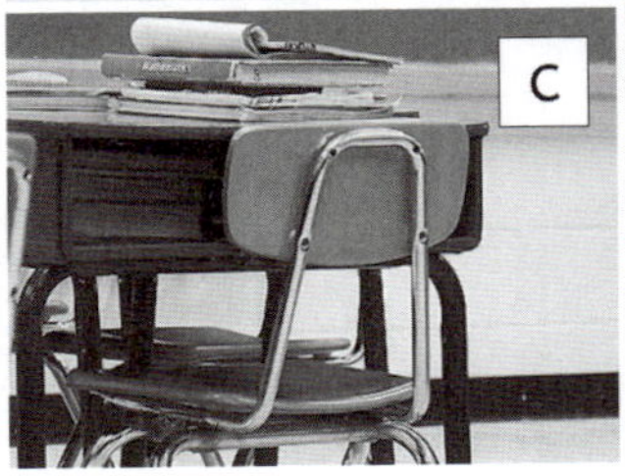

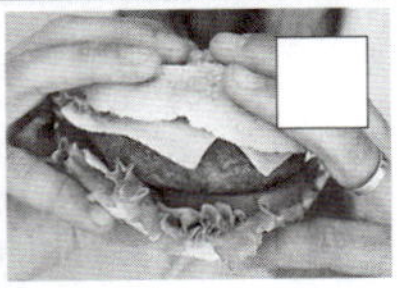

86 a Would you like **some** milk in your coffee?
b Rachel doesn't eat **any** meat.
c Hello, I'm back. Is **anybody** at home?
d They have **some** chickens in the garden.
e We don't have **anything** to eat this afternoon.
f My sandwich isn't in the fridge. **Somebody** ate it.
g Did **anybody** watch the film last night?
h Tom is reading **some** pages of his new book.
i Is there **any** cake left?
j Does **anybody** know the new song by B & C?
k She can give me **some** apples for free.
l I can see **somebody** walking through our garden.
m We don't know **anything** about our neighbours.

27
24
30
23
2
3
21
26
15
12
22
25
19
10
13
9
33
18
16
14
11
36
29
5
20
4
8
6
35
28
7
17
1
31
32

87

CARFNE
France
TUKEYR
Turkey
NANGELD
England
EGERCE
Greece
ILAYT
Italy
TNEHRLANDSE
the Netherlands
EMRAGYN
Germany
RUSIAS
Russia
SAPIN
Spain

88

I'm Susanne from Germany. At home we speak German.
My name is Lara. My mother is from Brazil and my father is from Italy. He teaches me a bit of Italian.
I'm Peter from Ireland. My grand-dad teaches me Irish.
I'm José and I can speak Spanish because I'm from Spain.
I'm Olga from Russia. Besides English I can speak Russian.
I'm Joel from France and I can speak French.
I'm Giorgios. My father is from England, but my mother is from Greece. So I can also speak a little bit of Greek.

89 MARIE: Ich vermisse das deutsche Essen.
DAN: **She's missing the German food.**
JAMES: Doesn't she like any sausages and beans?
DAN: **Magst du keine Würste und Bohnen?**
MARIE: Ich esse kein Fleisch. Bohnen sind aber in Ordnung.
DAN: **She doesn't eat (any) meat. Beans are OK for her.**
LISA: Frage James, ob er etwas Obst oder Joghurt möchte.
DAN: **Would you like some fruit or yoghurt?**
JAMES: I'd like some fruit.
DAN: **Er hätte gerne Obst.**
LISA: O.k., dann hole ich etwas Obst für ihn und natürlich auch für dich.
DAN: Dankeschön!

Topic 11: Training for the competition

90 a **He should go jogging every day.**

b **He could have chicken and rice with vegetables.**

c

☐ ☐ ☑

d James must drink a lot of **water**.

e

☐ ☐ ☑

f

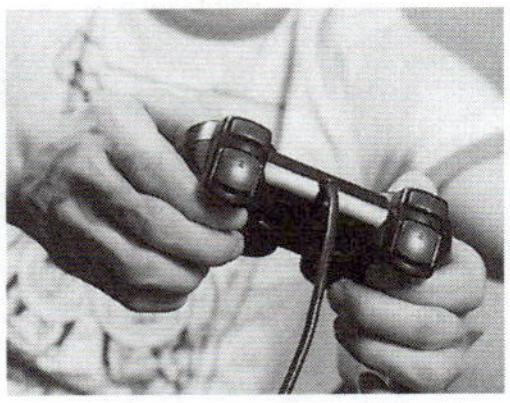

☐ ☑ ☐

91 **a** "I could go to basketball practice. It's on Tuesdays and Fridays."
"You could go to (basketball) practice on Tuesdays and Thursdays."
b "Rice and vegetables would be good for lunch or dinner."
c "It's good to eat a lot of food in the evening."
"You shouldn't have a big dinner late in the evening."
d "It's better to exercise alone."
"You could ask a friend to exercise with you."
e "Being on the Internet for too long isn't good."
f "I shouldn't go running daily." **"You should go jogging every day."**
g "I mustn't eat any sweets." **"You mustn't eat too many sweets."**

92 **a** My father could run very fast when he was young.
b I could also go by train.
c We could go swimming.
d James couldn't do his homework.
e I could see the Queen.
f Could you open the door, please?

93 **a** After school **I would go jogging** with a friend.
b James asked his friend Peter, **"Would you like to go jogging with me?"**
c I **would ask my sister** to play basketball with me.
d I **wouldn't exercise** when it's raining.
e James, I **wouldn't take part** in this competition.
f We **wouldn't do too much sport** in one day.

94 Man darf keine Straßenschuhe in der Sporthalle tragen.
Man muss seine Tasche in der Umkleidekabine lassen.
Man darf während des Trainings das Handy nicht benutzen.
Besucher müssen vor der Turnhalle (Sporthalle) warten.
Man muss zum Trainieren ein Handtuch benutzen.

95 Last week I **had to do** so much for school. Mr Smith gave us a history text and we **had to read** it in just two days. My mum says I **must/have to work/study** hard because my marks are not very good this year. I **mustn't get** a bad mark in the next maths test.
I normally **don't have to tidy up** in the kitchen, but mum was away for the weekend. So Tessa and I cleaned the kitchen. On warm days we both **have to help** in the garden, but I **mustn't cut** the bushes. Mum says it is too dangerous.

96 *Lösungsbeispiele:*

He should eat tomatoes, but he shouldn't eat pizza.
He should eat bananas, but he shouldn't eat muffins.
He should drink orange juice, but he shouldn't drink coke.
He should eat yoghurt, but he shouldn't eat chips.
He should eat potatoes, but he shouldn't eat sweets.
He should drink water, but he shouldn't drink lemonade.

97

picture	English	German
a	**do the laundry**	**die Wäsche waschen**
b	**iron clothes**	**die Kleidung bügeln**
c	**hoover the floor**	**den Boden saugen**
d	**prepare a meal**	**das Essen/eine Mahlzeit zubereiten**
e	**lay the table**	**den Tisch decken**
f	**take the rubbish out**	**den Müll raustragen**

98

Lösungswort: **DREAMHOUSE**

99 *Lösungsbeispiele:*
At the weekend I have to help my grandma. I have to go shopping for her.
I should make my bed every morning, but I don't do it.
Mum says I must tidy up my room every day.
I often have to take the rubbish out.
In the evening I have to do my homework.

Topic 12: The fortune teller

100

		true	false	not in the text
a	It's the last weekend before school starts again.	☐	☑	☐
b	At the fair you can also go swimming.	☐	☐	☑
c	Madame Wonder tells the future for £4.	☑	☐	☐
d	Tessa goes into the tent with Robby.	☐	☑	☐
e	The fortune teller has got a black cat.	☐	☐	☑
f	Robby will go on holiday with his parents.	☐	☐	☑
g	Tessa orders two hamburgers with chips.	☐	☑	☐
h	Tessa hasn't got enough money for lunch.	☑	☐	☐

101 Tessa and Robby are at a fair. **(f)**
Tessa wants to know about her future. **(o)**
Madame Wonder tells Tessa about her future. **(r)**
Tessa has to pay £4. **(t)**
Robby and Tessa are hungry and want to have lunch. **(u)**
Tessa doesn't have enough money. **(n)**
Robby pays for Tessa's hamburger. **(e)**

Lösungswort: **fortune**

102
a Tessa will sleep on the sofa tonight.
b She won't watch TV.
c Tessa will meet her favourite star.
d She will paint a picture.
e Tessa won't break her leg.
f Tessa won't tidy up her room.
g She will go inline skating tomorrow.

103
- **a** Will you go to Australia some day? – Yes, **I will.**
- **b** Will you be together with Eric? – No, **I won't.**
- **c** Will we always be friends? – **Yes, we will.**
- **d** Will you have a fast car? – **No, I won't.**
- **e** Will you have children? – **Yes, I will.**
- **f** Will we stay in Greenwich after school? – **No, we won't.**

104 *Lösungsbeispiele:*
- **a** When will we go to the swimming pool?
- **b** What will the tickets cost?
- **c** Why won't we have a picnic?
- **d** Who will buy a present for Peter's birthday?
- **e** Where will we meet?

105

106 *Lösungsbeispiel:*
On my dream holiday I will fly to Brazil with my best friend. We will sleep in a tree house in the middle of the jungle. During the day we will play with the baby monkeys and will eat bananas and coconuts.

Bildnachweis

Umschlag: © Stuart Pearcey/Dreamstime.com

Illustrationen S. 23, 24, 29, 31, 58, 59, 60, 63: © Rebecca Meyer;
sonstige Illustrationen: Stark Verlag

S. 1: © Adrienne Murphy/Dreamstime.com; S. 2: © Monkey Business Images/Dreamstime.com, © Jarenwicklund/Dreamstime.com, © Ft_photography/Dreamstime.com; S. 3: © Roman Sakhno/ Dreamstime.com, © Alan Rainbow-www.sxc.hu, © Hugolacasse/Dreamstime.com, © Skopal/ Dreamstime.com, © Tatyana Gladskikh/Dreamstime.com, © Hanns Christoph Merkle (www.hc-merkle.de)-www.sxc.hu, © Krzyssagit/Dreamstime.com, © Holger Karius/Dreamstime.com, © Paul Jenkinson; S. 4: © Dirk Schumann-Fotolia.com; S. 8: © Nicemonkey-Fotolia.com; S. 9: © Deminos-Fotolia.com, ©Anderson5cai/Dreamstime.com, © Warren0909/Dreamstime.com, © Elena Elisseeva/ Dreamstime.com; S. 10: © Greenland/Dreamstime.com, © fotodesign-jegg.de-Fotolia.com, © Haizul/ Dreamstime.com; S. 11: © Igor Zakowski-Fotolia.com; S. 12: © Juan Moyano/Dreamstime.com, © Ljupco Smokovski/Dreamstime.com, © Hongqi Zhang/Dreamstime.com; S. 13: © Photodo51-Fotolia.com, © Joanne Zh/Dreamstime.com, © Keung1616/Dreamstime.com, © Joe Gough/Dreamstime.com, © Sean Tunn/Dreamstime.com, © Imagestore/Dreamstime.com, © Olga Mirenska /Dreamstime.com, © Miflippo/ Dreamstime.com, ©Alex Bramwell/Dreamstime.com, © Pengdevey/Dreamstime.com, © Clearviewstock/Dreamstime.com, © Jonathan Ross/Dreamstime.com; S. 15: © Pengdevey/Dreams-time.com, © Monkey Business Images/Dreamstime.com, © Anna Jurkovska/Dreamstime.com; S. 16: © Dmitriy Shironosov/Dreamstime.com, © Monkey Business Images/Dreamstime.com, © Jacek Cha-braszewski/Dreamstime.com; S. 18: © Eric Ortner-sxc.hu; S. 19: © Klavapuk/Dreamstime.com; S. 20: © Keung1616/Dreamstime.com, © Nikolay Mamluke/Dreamstime.com, © Denis Babenko/Dreams-time.com, © Hupeng/Dreamstime.com, © Monkey Business Images/Dreamstime.com, © Lisa F. Young/ Dreamstime.com, © Araraadt/Dreamstime.com, © Knud Nielsen/Dreamstime.com, © Jov43/Dreams-time.com; S. 22: © Stuart Key/Dreamstime.com; S. 24: © Antondesign/Dreamstime.com; S. 28: © Orlan-do Florin Rosu/Dreamstime.com, © Ivan Bliznetsov/Dreamstime.com; © ilco-www.sxc.hu; S. 31: © Loo-pall/Dreamstime.com; S. 32: © dispicture-Fotolia.com, © Victoo/Dreamstime.com; S. 34: © Ivan Kmit/ Dreamstime.com, © Arne9001/Dreamstime.com, © Anna Dudko/Dreamstime.com, © Jan Martin Will/Dreamstime.com, © Walter Quirtmair/Dreamstime.com, © Kati Molin/Dreamstime.com, © Alexander Ishchenko/Dreamstime.com; S. 36: © Norman Pogson/Dreamstime.com; S. 37: © Matthew Benoit/Dreamstime.com; S. 38: © Redaktion, © nkzs-www.sxc.hu, © ftibor/www.sxc.hu, © Pascal THAU-VIN-sxc.hu, © Chode/Dreamstime.com, © Gabriela F. Ruellan/www.sxc.hu, ©Andrey Ananyn/Dreams-time.com, © Andre-Fotolia.com, © Marta Dehnel/www.sxc.hu; S. 39: © Jeka84/Dreamstime.com; S. 40: © Gary718/Dreamstime.com; S. 41: © Fotograf: Andreas F. Borchert; http://en.wikipedia.org/wiki/ File:Kilbennan_St._Benin's_Church_Window_St._Patrick_Detail_2010_09_16.jpg; lizenziert unter der Creative Commons Attribution-Share Alike 3.0 Germany license, © Fotograf: Dan Parsons; http://en.wiki-pedia.org/wiki/File:Apple_pie.jpg; lizenziert unter der Creative Commons Attribution-Share Alike 2.0 Generic license; © Gary718/Dreamstime.com, © Christophe Testi/Dreamstime.com, © John Loader/ Dreamstime.com; S. 44: © Elenathewise-Fotolia.com, © Ljupco Smokovski/Dreamstime.com,© Peter Close/Dreamstime.com, © Paul Jenkinson, © Marek Kosmal-Fotolia.com; S. 45: © Cybernesco/Dreams-time.com, © Yobro10/Dreamstime.com, © Peter Close/Dreamstime.com; S. 46: © Stanislaff/Dreams-time.com, © Michal Zacharzewski-sxc.hu, © Saniphoto/Dreamstime.com, © Ivonne Wierink/Dreams-time.com; S. 47: © Krzyssagit/Dreamstime.com, © Rene Pribil/Dreamstime.com,© Nelson Syozi-sxc.hu, © Jean Scheijen-www.vierdrie.nl/www.sxc.hu; S. 49: © Get4net/Dreamstime.com, © Hongqi Zhang/ Dreamstime.com, © Denis Radovanovic/Dreamstime.com; S. 50: © Ljupco Smokovski/Dreamstime.com, © Roman Borodaev/Dreamstime.com, © Heike Brauer/Dreamstime.com, © Otto Versand GmbH & Co KG, © Gemenacom/Dreamstime.com, © Denis Radovanovic/Dreamstime.com, © Get4net/Dreams-time.com, © Pgaborphotos/Dreamstime.com; S. 57: © Iwona joanna Rajszczak/Dreamstime.com; S. 58: © Rldcstock/Dreamstime.com; S. 60: © Marion Augenstein; S. 61: © Konstantin Kamenetskiy/Dreams-time.com, © Edward J Bock 111/Dreamstime.com, © Jürgen Scharp-Fotolia.com, © Alix Marina-Fotolia.com, © Fotomenne-Fotolia.com, © Oleksii Sagitov/Dreamstime.com, © Roberto A. Sanchez-www.istockfoto.com, © Mulltiart61/Dreamstime.com, © Ginasanders/Dreamstime.com; S. 62: © Pokerman/Dreamstime.com; S. 64: © Vvvstep/Dreamstime.com; S. 66: © Luba V Nel/Dreams-time.com; S. 67: © Garsya/Dreamstime.com; S. 70: © Soland/Dreamstime.com; © Taylor Jackson/ Dreamstime.com; © Artcp5/Dreamstime.com; S. 71: © Irochka/Dreamstime.com; S. 72: © Sandy38/

Dreamstime.com; © Monkey Business Images/Dreamstime.com; © Keung1616/Dreamstime.com; © Barbara Reddoch/Dreamstime.com; © jamunab-Fotolia.com; S. 73: © Chad Mcdermott/Dreamstime.com; S. 74: © brokenarts-sxc.hu; S. 76: © ISO K-photography-Fotolia.com; © ehrenberg-bilder-Fotolia.com; © west-Fotolia.com; S. 77: © Ivan Kmit/Dreamstime.com; S. 78: © Mehmet Uluç Ceylani/Dreamstime.com; © Norman Pogson/Dreamstime.com; © Matthew Benoit/ Dreamstime.com; S. 79: © Redaktion; © Rafael Angel Irusta Machin/Dreamstime.com; © Roman Milert/Dreamstime.com; © Jiri Hera/Dreamstime.com; © Egahen/www.sxc.hu; © Mauhorng/Dreamstime.com; © Miodrag Gajic/Dreamstime.com;© Anke Van Wyk/Dreamstime.com; © Ileanaolaru/Dreamstime.com; S. 81: © Diego Vito Cervo/Dreamstime.com; © Simon Krzic/Dreamstime.com; © Glen Jones-Fotolia.com; © Vvvstep/Dreamstime.com; © Monkey Business Images/Dreamstime.com; © Nikolay Okhitin/Dreamstime.com; S. 84: © Diademimages/Dreamstime.com; Bild Sultan Ahmed Moschee (gemeinfrei), © Shutter1970/Dreamstime.com; © Fotograf: Taxiarchos228; http://de.wikipedia.org/wiki/Datei:Parthenon_Athen.jpg; lizenziert unter der GNU-Lizenz für freie Dokumentation, Version 1.2 oder einer späteren Version, veröffentlicht von der Free Software Foundation, © Fotograf: Softeis; http://commons.wikimedia.org/wiki/File:Leaning_Tower_of_Pisa.jpg; lizenziert unter der GNU Free Documentation License, Version 1.2 or any later version published by the Free Software Foundation; Windmühlen (gemeinfrei), © Fotograf: Norbert Aepli, Switzerland; http://eo.wikipedia.org/wiki/Dosiero:Brandenburger_Tor_2005_006.JPG; lizenziert unter CC-BY-2.5; © Fotograf: A.Savin; http://de.wikipedia.org/wiki/Datei:Basil-cathedral-morning.jpg; lizenziert unter der GNU-Lizenz für freie Dokumentation, Version 1.2 oder einer späteren Version, veröffentlicht von der Free Software Foundation, © http://commons.wikimedia.org/wiki/File:Toro_de_Osborne_BIG.JPG, lizenziert unter der GNU Free Documentation License, Version 1.2 or any later version published by the Free Software Foundation, © Jov43/Dreamstime.com; S. 85: © Monkey Business Images/Dreamstime.com; S. 86: © Monkey Business Images/Dreamstime.com; S. 87: © Marcelmooij/Dreamstime.com; S. 88: © Marc Dietrich/Dreamstime.com; © Jean Scheijen/sxc.hu; © Mariia Gerasymenko/Dreamstime.com; © Saniphoto/ Dreamstime.com; © Philip Lange/Dreamstime.com; © Diego Cervo/Dreamstime.com; S. 93© Garsya/Dreamstime.com; S. 94: © Dan Race-Fotolia.com; © Monkey Business Images/Dreamstime.com; © Balázs Justin/Dreamstime.com; © Isabel Poulin/Dreamstime.com; © Ingrid Balabanova /Dreamstime.com; © GordonGrand-Fotolia.com; S. 95: © 1000words/ Dreamstime.com; © Mailthepic/Dreamstime.com; © Brett Critchley/ Dreamstime.com; S. 97: © Darrenw/Dreamstime.com; © Kelpfish/Dreamstime.com; S. 99: © Bowie15/ Dreamstime.com; S. 100: © Greenland/Dreamstime.com; © Lunamarina/Dreamstime.com; © Jacek Chabraszewski/Dreamstime.com; S. 101: © Kameel4u/ Dreamstime.com; © Monkey Business Images/Dreamstime.com; © Donkeyru/Dreamstime.com; S. 102: © Ljupco Smokovski/Dreamstime.com; © Suzanne Tucker/Dreamstime.com; S. 104: © Cheryl Casey/Dreamstime.com; © Iakov Filimonov/Dreamstime.com; © Kelley.garner/Dreamstime.com; © Softdreams/ Dreamstime.com; © Studio 37/Dreamstime.com; © Christa Eder-Fotolia.com; © Dmitry Ersler/Fotolia.com; S. 105: © Konstik/Dreamstime.com; S. 107: Young Kimpark/Dreamstime.com; S. 119: Les Cunliffe/Dreamstime.com

Quellennachweis

Text S. 11 und 120: "My Dog Does My Homework" copyright © 2004 Kenn Nesbitt. All Rights Reserved. Reprinted by permission of the author.

Ihre Meinung ist uns wichtig!

Ihre Anregungen sind uns immer willkommen. Bitte informieren Sie uns mit diesem Schein über Ihre Verbesserungsvorschläge!

Titel-Nr.	Seite	Vorschlag

Bitte hier abtrennen

Zutreffendes bitte ankreuzen!

Die Absenderin/der Absender ist:

- ☐ Lehrer/in in den Klassenstufen: ______
- ☐ Fachbetreuer/in
  Fächer: ______
- ☐ Seminarlehrer/in
  Fächer: ______
- ☐ Regierungsfachberater/in
  Fächer: ______
- ☐ Oberstufenbetreuer/in
- ☐ Schulleiter/in
- ☐ Referendar/in, Termin 2. Staatsexamen: ______
- ☐ Leiter/in Lehrerbibliothek
- ☐ Leiter/in Schülerbibliothek
- ☐ Sekretariat
- ☐ Eltern
- ☐ Schüler/in, Klasse: ______
- ☐ Sonstiges: ______

Unterrichtsfächer: (Bei Lehrkräften!)

______

STARK Verlag
Postfach 1852
85318 Freising

22-VTX
Bitte ausfüllen und im frankierten Umschlag an uns einsenden. Für Fensterkuverts geeignet.

Kennen Sie Ihre Kundennummer?
Bitte hier eintragen.

Absender (Bitte in Druckbuchstaben!)

Name/Vorname

Straße/Nr.

PLZ/Ort/Ortsteil

Telefon privat

Geburtsjahr

E-Mail

Schule/Schulstempel (Bitte immer angeben!)

Bitte hier abtrennen

(Bitte blättern Sie um)